Human Systems and the Environment
An INTERLAB Series
Frederick L. Bates, General Editor

The series is dedicated to expanding our knowledge of
sociopolitical and sociocultural ecology, the study of the
relation between human systems and the environment from the
perspective of the social sciences. Individual volumes will
address the social, cultural, political, and economic
dimensions of environmental problems.

Human Systems and the Environment

Living Conditions, Disasters, and Development

Living Conditions, Disasters, and Development

An Approach to Cross-Cultural Comparisons

Frederick L. Bates and Walter Gillis Peacock

In collaboration with Carlos Aramburu, Manuel Esparza,
Aydin Germen, Dennis Mileti, Josip Obradovic, Carlo Pelanda

The University of Georgia Press   /   Athens and London

Paperback edition, 2008
© 1993 by the University of Georgia Press
Athens, Georgia 30602
www.ugapress.org
All rights reserved
Set in 10/13 Times Roman by Tseng Information Systems, Inc.
Printed digitally in the United States of America

The Library of Congress has cataloged the hardcover edition
of this book as follows:

Library of Congress Cataloging-in-Publication Data

Bates, Frederick L.
    Living conditions, disasters, and development : an approach to cross-
cultural comparisons / Frederick L. Bates and Walter Gillis Peacock in
collaboration with Carlos Aramburu . . . [et al.].
        xiv, 159 p. ; 24 cm.
    (Human systems and the environment)
    ISBN 0-8203-1484-6 (alk. paper)
    Includes bibliographical references (p. 151-156) and index.
    1. Disasters–Economic aspects–Cross-cultural studies. 2. Cost and
standard of living–Cross-cultural studies. 3. Household appliances–Cross-
cultural studies. 4. Crisis management–Cross-cultural studies. 5. Survival
skills–Cross-cultural studies. I. Peacock, Walter Gillis. II. Title. III. Series:
Human systems and the environment
HC79.D45 B38   1993
338.9 20   92-5379

Paperback ISBN-13: 978-0-8203-3122-5
ISBN-10: 0-8203-3122-8

British Library Cataloging-in-Publication Data available

To the Guatemalans who, through their collaboration with us as participants in the Guatemalan Earthquake Project, contributed heavily to the development of the Domestic Assets Scale and who have since perished in the struggle to improve their own living conditions

Contents

Tables

Preface

This monograph has grown out of a group effort that extends back well over ten years. During that time many people contributed both theoretical and methodological ideas, and many worked in the field to apply these ideas in interviews with households in seven different countries. The work began in Guatemala in the late 1970s in connection with the Guatemalan Earthquake Study. During that research, a slightly modified Belcher cross-cultural level of living scale, along with a damage estimation technique, was used to measure disaster impact at the household level. In that study about 1,500 households in 26 villages and urban neighborhoods were interviewed in three waves using the cross-cultural level of living technique to measure progress toward recovery once disaster losses have been estimated.

The Belcher method was eventually modified by using monetary weights as the means of arriving at a *modified level of living score*. To distinguish it from the Belcher method, the name of the scale was changed to the *Domestic Assets Scale*.

The method seemed so promising that funds were sought and received from the National Science Foundation (Grant no. CES 872742) to extend the work begun in Guatemala by modifying the scale further and testing it in a variety of socioeconomic and cultural settings. This monograph is the result of that second effort.

The original Guatemalan research team included Frederick L. Bates as principal investigator and W. Timothy Farrell and JoAnn K. Glittenberg as co-principal investigators. Thomas Edwards served as field director, managing a team of six Guatemalan interviewers. Extremely important to the successful formulation and completion of this project were the two graduate research assistants, Charles D. Killian and Walter Gillis Peacock. Much of the theoretical work on the project and virtually all of the difficult and complex computer analysis was conducted by these two individuals in close collaboration with the principal investigator. Hettie Dowtin Bates was project secretary throughout this effort and helped manage the project's complex international business affairs as well as its logistics and manuscript production.

During the six-country study on which this book reports, Frederick Bates acted as principal investigator and Peacock as co-principal investigator. In the early phases, Killian collaborated with them in developing the research plan and in designing and producing the interview schedules and manuals.

Daniel G. Rodeheaver, who had collaborated with the research team in the later stages of the Guatemalan Earthquake Study, continued to work on the six-country study, especially in conducting a field test of the instrument in Mexico City following the 1985 earthquake there.

In the research for this project, absolutely indispensable roles were played by the six collaborating scholars listed on the title page. These were Carlos Aramburu in Peru, Manuel Esparza in Mexico, Aydin Germen in Turkey, Dennis Mileti in the United States, Josip Obradovic in Yugoslavia, and Carlo Pelanda in Italy. They not only managed the fieldwork in their own countries, but in a succession of meetings and by mail and telephone, as well as in field visits from the principal investigator, they contributed heavily to the theoretical foundation of the Domestic Assets Scale and to the methodology for its application. We are deeply indebted to them for their willingness to participate and for the thorough and diligent manner with which they conducted the field operations.

While this monograph is the culmination of a truly group effort by 15 or 20 people and was supported by the National Science Foundation, its present form and contents are the responsibility of the two principal authors.

Living Conditions, Disasters, and Development

Chapter 1

The Cross-Cultural Measurement of Disaster Impact on Household Living Conditions and Its Relationship to Development

Social science research into the impact of and human response to disaster has a long history reaching back at least to the seminal study by Samuel H. Prince (1925) of the Halifax disaster. Regardless of its particular focus, this research almost always requires the use of some measure that assesses a disaster's impact on some population of social units chosen as the object of investigation. The type of measure employed depends on the objective of the research and on the type of unit used as the basis of observation (Quarentelli 1978; Drabek 1986). In almost every case, however, there is a need to assess the change in some variable or set of variables that measures the impact of the disaster agent on some attribute or set of attributes of the unit under investigation so that the research can estimate the disaster's effects as a physical event and can measure subsequent recovery processes. Such a measure is most often used as a dependent variable in research aimed at explaining or understanding the impact of a disaster in social and physical terms as well as in the social processes determining recovery.

For example, if the study is aimed at examining the impact of a disaster on the mental health of individuals exposed to it, the measure will obviously be designed to assess mental health effects and the unit of investigation will normally be the individual (Wilson 1962; Bates et al. 1963; Kreps 1984). If the objective is to understand how a disaster disrupts and disorganizes the operation of normal community-level institutions, the measure will be designed around variables or attributes that are believed to operationalize community-level impact and recovery—for example, business failures and starts (Bates and Peacock 1987; Hoover and Bates 1986; Wenger 1978; Wright et al. 1979; Friesema et al. 1979). It is even possible that the unit of analysis could be an entire society or nation, in which case the focus would be on factors such as the national economy assessed by gross domestic production and the like (Abril-Ojeda 1982). Clearly, then, the measure employed depends on the research problem and on

1

how that problem is conceptualized. It is apparent that no single measure of disaster impact can serve all purposes.

Since no single measure will suffice, social scientists find a need to develop and test a set of standardized disaster impact measures that are ready for use well before a disaster study is undertaken. The nature of disasters and disaster research is such that the researcher usually has little time to design, pretest, and validate research instruments, especially those aspects of data collection protocols that elicit the information necessary for use in creating relatively precise, valid, and reliable instruments to assess disaster impact (Mileti et al. 1975; Mileti 1987). Disasters by their nature are relatively rare, geographically dispersed, unscheduled events (Fritz 1961; Baker and Chapman 1962). Many types of disasters develop rapidly, and the initial impact phase is over before the researcher is able to get into the field, meaning that the pre-disaster and early emergency phases must be reconstructed on the basis of retrospective interviews and documentary evidence, even when the research response is quite prompt. The existence of a tool kit of pretested research instruments that contains standardized measures of key variables would therefore greatly facilitate and improve disaster research. Aside from facilitating the promptness of research response, such standardized measures would improve the comparability of research conducted by different researchers and allow results from many different studies to add up to a better understanding of the disaster process (Bates and Peacock 1992).

The research described in this monograph was directed toward creating and field-testing one such standardized measure of disaster impact, which, it is hoped, can be used by researchers interested in studying the effects on household living conditions of large, physically destructive events. It was undertaken on the assumption that disaster impact measures should be usable cross-culturally and that they should yield a measure which would allow researchers to compare results obtained from studies conducted in societies with wide cultural differences and with pronounced differences in levels of economic development.

Because disasters are relatively rare in any given society, long-run progress in understanding the disaster process as a social phenomenon requires that researchers be able to compare the results of studies conducted in different social and cultural settings. It also requires them to compare results obtained from the study of different types of disasters. For example, disaster researchers must be able to compare the social impact of hurricanes, tornadoes, earthquakes, floods, and perhaps physically destructive technological or man-made disasters if they are to understand the relationship between disasters as physical events and as social phenomena. The aim of the research reported here, therefore, was to create a cross-cultural, cross-disaster measure that would accurately assess the impact of a physical event on households as social units, using household living conditions as the impact indicator.

Theoretical Background

Disasters can have a variety of impacts on households, causing the death of members, psychological stress, and economic loss. In light of the multidimensional nature of these impacts, researchers have attempted to assess both subjective sociopsychological and more objective impacts (Hill and Hansen 1962; Drabek 1986). Measures have included psychological tests designed to assess subjective feelings of loss and stress to more objective measures such as losses in income, housing, and household possessions (Bolin 1976, 1982; Bolin and Trainer 1978; Bates 1982; Bolin and Bolton 1983; Hultåker and Trost 1983; and Peacock, Killian, and Bates 1987). Objective measures draw on the observation that one important way in which physically destructive disasters affect households is by altering their living conditions. The following research focuses on this fact and utilizes a conceptualization of living conditions and their relationship to household functioning as a basis for creating a cross-cultural, cross-disaster impact measure.

For purposes of this research, living conditions are defined as the set of physical facilities employed by the household group to perform ordinary household functions and to satisfy the needs of members for shelter, personal hygiene, sanitation, food preparation and consumption, sleeping, and so forth. Physical living conditions amount to the collection of possessions that provide the technological equipment used by the household group to carry on daily household activities. In this study, the concept of physical living conditions is restricted to consideration of the housing unit occupied by the household group and its contents, including the tools and equipment it uses to perform household functions such as cooking and clothes washing. The concept also includes the furnishings that households employ for dining and sleeping, utilities to furnish energy and water supply, and those items of technology for sanitation, such as bathtubs and toilets.

This research rests on several assumptions concerning the relationship between disasters and living conditions and between living conditions and sociocultural differences. These need to be discussed before the methodology employed in this study can be understood.

Relationship Between Disasters
and Household Living Conditions

Disasters that involve the sudden release of energy can result in a large physical impact on man-made structures, damaging and destroying the physical setting within which normal human activities are carried on. Human behavior systems at all levels, extending from households through work organization to community and societal social systems, employ a physical technology to carry on their normal patterns of activity (Lenski 1966; Lenski, Lenski, and Nolan 1991). When these items of technology are damaged, destroyed, or made inoperative, the normal pattern of functioning is disrupted. This disruption and its consequences constitute the disaster as a social rather than a physical event (Bates and Peacock 1987).

After a disaster with a high physical impact, normal activity patterns cannot be resumed until the physical setting, on which regular, daily activity depends, is restored; this process often seems to occur in phases, or stages (Barton 1963; Mileti et al. 1975). Therefore, much of the activity that follows a disaster is directed toward reconstructing the physical setting. Once the emergency is over and such vital activities as caring for the injured, rescuing those trapped in the rubble, and managing life-threatening situations such as fires and dangerous infrastructural conditions have been taken care of, attention turns to creating a set of temporary physical conditions to allow victims to survive and carry out vital activities while permanent reconstruction is carried out. Temporary shelters are created, the power and water systems are patched together, emergency food facilities and programs are organized, and other essentially temporary emergency measures are taken that substitute, for a time, for normal living conditions. Then the task of reconstruction begins. In cases where housing units have been damaged or destroyed, part of this process always involves efforts to restore household living conditions.

Given that disasters have an impact on the physical structure or technology needed and used to carry out normal activities, it seems reasonable that one can assess disaster impact by focusing on damage to these physical features. This means that one indicator of disaster impact at the household level can be obtained by measuring the degree to which physical living conditions have been disrupted. The reasoning is that the greater the destruction of living conditions, the greater the disruption of household activity patterns, and the greater the effort and resources necessary to restore those patterns.

A Cross-Cultural View of Living Conditions

There is a long history within the social sciences of attempts to develop measures assessing various concepts relating to household living conditions. For example, working groups under the auspices of the United Nations and the Rural Sociological Society have been concerned with measuring level and quality of living (Drewnowski 1970; Scott Wolf 1978; Charles P. Wolf 1979; Ad Hoc Committee 1956; UN Report 1953). Urban planners, economists, and sociologists are often interested in related concerns, including the development of measures of the quality of life (Terleckyj 1975; Morris 1979; Katzner 1979; Boulding 1984; and Andrews 1986). In addition, a host of other social scientists, including sociologists and anthropologists, have sought to develop measures of socioeconomic standing and/or level of living that overcome the limitations of using income alone to assess socioeconomic standing—especially in rural agricultural or semi-cash economies—and have relevance on a cross-cultural basis (Chapin 1938; Sewell 1940, 1943; Hagood and Ducoff 1944; Ramsey and Collazo 1960; Sharp and Ramsey 1963; Ugalde 1970; Knox 1974).

Our research draws on aspects of this work, in particular those studies that focus more specifically on measuring level of living; but it also seeks to overcome some limitations inherent in many of these approaches. For example, a major problem in many attempts to measure living conditions has been a failure to specify and clearly delineate a theoretical foundation on which the measure rests. As a result, many but not all of the resulting measures lack a coherent theoretical structure and are of limited utility in longitudinal or cross-cultural research. The chapters to follow will elucidate the theoretical assumptions guiding the development of our measure and discuss its strengths over many of the aforementioned approaches.

This research is based on the assumption that in every society, no matter what its culture or level of economic and technological development, households utilize a set of physical facilities and equipment to carry on daily activities. In order to establish and maintain a household, a group of people have to acquire a set of physical items that are employed to carry out activities which perform normal household functions. Furthermore, a set of functions appears to be characteristic of households in virtually every society. For example, households everywhere provide themselves with the physical items necessary for (1) shelter, (2) water, (3) food preservation and protection, (4) food preparation, (5) food serving and consumption, (6) sleeping, (7) human waste disposal, (8) bathing, (9) washing of clothes, dishes, and utensils, (10) lighting, (11) climate control, and (12) communications.

What differs from one society to another, depending on culture and level of economic development, is the type of physical item or items employed to perform a given function. Furthermore, within a given society, households at various economic levels will differ in the type and quality of the item they employ to perform a given function (Sobel 1981, 1983). For example, in economically advanced societies, food will be cooked on gas or electric stoves or in microwave ovens by even the middle and lower classes, but in less-developed societies only the rich will employ such facilities, and the poor will cook their food on open fires set in fireplaces on the floor or on stoves that use wood or other "natural" fuels. In between the rich and poor are many possible alternative types of cooking devices.

Thus, while cooking is a common function, the thing that varies from society to society and from economic stratum to stratum within a society is the type of device employed to carry out that function. This observation was noted by John C. Belcher (1972) when he devised his cross-cultural level of living scale. He pointed out that it is possible to measure the socioeconomic level of a household in any society, relative to other members of the same society, and relative to households in other societies, by determining the kinds of physical facilities or equipment they use to perform a standard set of household functions.

On this basis, Belcher claimed that two households taken from different societies which employ similar technologies to perform a set of common functions would have the same level of living. He further held that items of household technology employed by different households to perform the same function could be ranked according to *technological efficiency* and that higher levels of technological efficiency yielded higher levels of living. The implied reasoning is that higher levels of efficiency are related to such things as the amount of drudgery or hard physical labor required to perform a task and in many cases to exposure to health hazards that are often associated with sanitation and exposure to the elements. For example, with respect to cooking, gas and electric stoves not only require less human effort than open fires located on the floor of a dwelling unit, but they do not release smoke into the unit, and they cook food at a hotter, more even temperature, thus destroying waterborne bacteria, amoeba, and other disease-producing elements. As a consequence, it can be argued that a household which uses a technologically advanced method of cooking enjoys a higher level of living than one that does not.

Belcher reasoned that if a set of common functions could be found for virtually all households, no matter what their society's culture and no matter what its levels of economic development, and if an exhaustive inventory of all possible types of equipment used to perform each function could be obtained, then a cross-cultural level of living scale could be devised. The scale would work by rating the technological efficiency of each item employed to perform each function, relative to other items used to perform that same function; then, a score would be assigned to a household on how it ranked on each function with respect to the item it used to perform that function. The total score for a household would consist of the summed total of the scores given on each item. Thus, an extremely poor household that uses the crudest technology to perform all household functions would receive a low score, simultaneously representing a low level of technological efficiency in performing household functions and a low level of living. The Belcher approach may be called the *functional efficiency approach* to creating a level of living scale since it seeks cross-cultural validity by using functional areas as the means of achieving comparability and uses an estimate of technological efficiency to furnish a metric for scaling the underlying variable. Several of its advantages over standard level of living scales make it interesting for use in studies of socioeconomic development and for disaster research.

Unlike standard level of living scales, the Belcher scale allows social and economic change to be measured over both relatively short and long periods, and it allows this measurement on a cross-cultural basis. Standard level of living scales obtain information on the possession or nonpossession of physical items that are known at a given historical time to differentiate between households with high and low economic status (e.g., Sewell 1940, 1943; Sharp and Ramsey 1963). The items employed are usually those that represent the upper end of the scale of technological advancement, and households are rated according to how many of these items they possess. For example, households today might be rated on these items:

1. More than two bathrooms?
2. A guest bedroom used for no other purpose?
3. A refrigerator with automatic ice maker and water dispenser?
4. An automatic programmable washing machine and dryer?
5. An electric or gas stove or oven with programmable controls?
6. A microwave oven?
7. A high fidelity stereo player capable of using digital recordings?
8. A color television set with a screen larger than 24 inches?
9. A video tape recorder?
10. A personal computer?

The difficulty with such scales is that they are useful only for a short time, especially in societies that are changing relatively rapidly (Sewell 1943; Sharp and Ramsey 1963). Items on the original level of living scales used in the United States in the 1930s are of virtually no value today in differentiating between the socioeconomic status of households. In the 1930s, the items employed were such things as "Do you have running water, a flush toilet, electricity, a radio, etc?" Today, virtually every U.S. household possesses these items, and they do not differentiate between upper, middle, and lower socioeconomic groups. In the same way, scales that depend on the most advanced items to differentiate between the rich and the poor in the United States, Western Europe, and Japan will fail to differentiate within a low-income society where only a small number of the most affluent will possess these items.

In contrast, the Belcher approach allows differentiation along all levels of socioeconomic development since it obtains information on the most primitive as well as the most advanced technologies. This approach can not only differentiate within and between societies, but it can measure change, since a household can move up or down the scale as it acquires more advanced technology or is forced to use more primitive means of performing household functions as a result of losses incurred in a disaster.

Another advantage of a scale such as this one is that it is capable of measuring differences in level of living among households in even the most economically deprived community, and it can place households in such communities on a scale relative to households in the most affluent and technologically advanced communities. Households who live in straw houses, cook their food on open fires on the floor, obtain their water supply from a river, have no bathing facilities, and wash their clothes in a stream can theoretically be placed on the same scale with households that live in expensive, multiroom dwellings with the most modern internal facilities.

To use this procedure, one must be willing to agree with Belcher's use of technological efficiency as the basic metric employed to score the items of technology. There are, however, some serious problems involved in accepting this method. First, it is not all that easy to rank items of technology in terms of efficiency. In some cases, Belcher seems to have used the amount of human labor required to employ the item as the basis for rating efficiency, and in others he seems to have used the capacity of the technology to provide sanitation, or hygiene, or protection from the environment. For example, an automatic washing machine is said to be more efficient than a washtub and scrub board because it requires less hard human labor, thus saving time and energy that can be devoted to other activities. But the washing machine also makes clothes cleaner and less subject to wear and tear. A central running water supply piped into the home from a safe water source is more efficient than carrying water in buckets or water jars from a lake or stream because it requires less household labor, but at the same time it avoids waterborne diseases.

Even if these assumptions can be agreed on, the question remains of how much more efficient are more capital-intensive advanced technologies than more labor-intensive ones? If the consumption of all types of energy were used to rate efficiency, labor-intensive technologies might easily prove more efficient. The manufacture of an automatic washing machine requires great expenditures of energy as one traces the processes from the extraction of raw resources to the machine's final assembly. If the total calories of energy used were measured, it would probably turn out that hand washing of clothes requires many fewer calories than using automatic washers and dryers.

Belcher simply ranked his items of technology for a given function on a five-point scale with equal distances between items (Bates, Killian, and Peacock 1984). Thus, an automatic washing machine received 5 points; a hand-filled wringer washer, 4 points; built-in household washtubs, 3 points; a public washing place furnished by the city for hand washing, 2 points; and washing in portable tubs or in a river or lake, 1 point. Each functional area was similarly handled with the most technologically efficient type of equipment receiving 5 points and the least efficient, 1 point. In addition, according to Belcher's logic, each functional area was given equal weight within the measure on the total scale. Therefore, to use the Belcher scale, one must be willing to accept the proposition that all functional areas are equally important to total level of living. In other words, the contribution of shelter to the overall scale is equivalent to clothes or dishwashing equipment. If, instead, one thinks housing is more important to living conditions than how clothes are washed and food is cooked, this scale will distort level of living in favor of relatively unimportant items of technology. Such a distortion may not operate equally between social classes in the same society or between societies with different levels of development.

Although the research reported here is based on Belcher's functional efficiency approach and is aimed at achieving cross-cultural comparability by using the items of technology employed to perform basic household functions as a means of measuring living conditions and ultimately for measuring disaster impact, it abandons the notion of technological efficiency as the underlying metric. In addition, the method of ranking items on a five-point scale and equal weighting of functional areas is abandoned. In particular, our approach substitutes the monetary cost of each item for level of technological efficiency. Thus, the method arrives at what can be called a cost-weighted scale. Subsequent chapters will deal with the specific modifications and their advantages introduced by this research. Before developing these specifics, however, the reasoning behind this strategy should be discussed.

The Use of Household Living Conditions as a Measure of Disaster Impact

To employ a level of living approach to measure disaster impact on households, a theoretical foundation is needed. This foundation should relate disasters to normal processes through which households establish a set of living conditions, and it also should be compatible with a conceptualization of the process of social and economic development by which societies evolve their typical modes of adaptation to their environment (Bates 1982; Bates and Peacock 1987, 1991; Rodeheaver 1990). In addition, it is important to understand how disasters are related to the developmental levels of the communities in which they occur.

Disasters as social phenomena are so closely related to the process of social and economic development that they cannot be understood without placing them in perspective with development (Bates 1982; Abril-Ojeda 1982; Bates and Peacock 1987, 1989; Rodeheaver 1990). This is especially true for this study, which attempts to deal with disasters from a cross-cultural perspective, making it mandatory to consider the relationship between disasters and the level of development of the societies they strike. In the process of dealing with these issues, it is necessary to relate a conceptualization of living conditions to both development and disasters since it is through this concept that our research attempts to provide a development-related, cross-cultural measure of disaster impact.

The best way to proceed is, first, to discuss development as an evolutionary process related to the establishment of a set of living conditions, and then to discuss how households in societies that have achieved a given level of living establish their personal set of living conditions. The first approach considers development as a process affecting whole societies, and the second considers how households within societies acquire their particular set of living conditions in the context of a society at a given level of development.

Development as a Process

Human societies and the various subsystems within them (for example, households) evolve to provide the behavior patterns that are used by a human population to adapt to each other and to an environment from which they draw the resources they employ to satisfy their needs and wants (Lenski 1966; Lenski,

Lenski, and Nolan 1991). Societies also evolve to provide adaptations to environmental conditions that threaten the population's survival. The long process of social evolution can be viewed as the way in which people have attempted to reduce their vulnerability to events and conditions that threaten their survival by developing a set of learned behavior patterns, the results of which are predictable when employed in adapting to their environment.

All animal species survive by employing behavior as a means of adaptation and as the mechanism to draw needed resources from the environment. An animal organism's challenge is to perform in ways that succeed in predicting the outcome of a transaction with the environment and that result in its survival. To survive, the organism must have a greater than chance probability of selecting a behavioral response to the environment that will succeed in drawing needed resources from the environment, or of protecting the organism against environmental conditions that threaten its continued existence.

At least two paths of evolution have succeeded in adapting animal organisms to their environments through the development of behavior patterns. First, there has been the hereditary route through which genetically transmitted behavior patterns have evolved within a species and been genetically transmitted to individual organisms within the species. In this case, biological evolution has produced organic mechanisms that supply adaptive behavior patterns. The second route has been through the use of learning and the development and accumulation of behavior patterns in the form of culture. In this case, which applies in the case of humans, organisms accumulate information through their experiences in an environment, and they convert that information into a set of cultural patterns that supply individual members, as well as the population as a whole, with adaptive patterns.

A detailed discussion of the processes by which learned behavior patterns evolve and develop is both impossible and unnecessary here. The important point is that culture may be regarded as a set of behavior patterns that have evolved to provide a human population's adaptation to an environment by reducing the uncertainty of its survival and, therefore, by reducing its vulnerability to uncontrolled, unexpected transactions with that environment.

This set of patterns develops out of interaction between the population and the environment and may be seen as a process whereby behavioral solutions that either succeed in reducing vulnerability or that are neutral with respect to vulnerability survive to be transmitted to the next generation. Those patterns that increase vulnerability and lead to nonsurvival are selected out as their users are overcome by conditions to which they cannot adapt. At any given moment in a human population's history, the contents of its culture consist of the adaptive patterns that until that point, have succeeded in assuring its survival through reducing vulnerability to the environmental conditions out of which the population evolved.

The fact that patterns exist does not mean that they are the best possible solutions to adaptation problems, in the long run, but only that they have proven to be within the limits of vulnerability to the set of environmental conditions that a given population has experienced until that moment. Furthermore, it must be recognized that these adaptive patterns, in order to survive and reproduce themselves, must only permit the population employing them to live long enough and to be in such a condition of organic health as to reproduce themselves, thus passing the patterns on to the next generation.

Some cultural patterns may yield environmental adaptations that result in maintaining small, stable populations, which survive over long periods by maintaining a precarious relationship with their environment (Lenski 1966; Lenski, Lenski, and Nolan 1991). Such an unstable relationship can easily be disturbed and can result, if environmental conditions change suddenly or radically, in overwhelming the population depending on it. Although the population survives, its level of survival involves harsh living conditions and high morbidity and mortality rates, which, if not balanced by high birthrates, result in catastrophe for the population. At the other end of the scale are cultural patterns that adapt a population to its environment by so reducing vulnerability to death rates that the population expands rapidly, for a time insuring not only its continuation but the survival of its adaptive cultural apparatus. Even so, undue success in assuring a population's survival that leads to rapid population expansion may have an impact on the environment and lead to future vulnerability stemming from resource depletion and environmental degradation or from conflicts with other populations over space and resources.

In order to understand differences in levels of development among coexisting societies, when it is assumed that all existing societies, because they exist, must provide a system of adaptation sufficiently successful to have survived into the present, it is necessary to examine the concept of vulnerability. The first step toward such an understanding, in the sociocultural sense, is to realize that every pattern of adaptation, no matter how technologically advanced or successful in relation to present conditions, is nevertheless vulnerable to certain environmental conditions that lie beyond, or outside, the range of conditions which that pattern evolved to deal with. This means that every adaptive pattern is subject to increased vulnerability as its environment changes or as rare and unusual events occur in that environment which its culture does not predict and for which it does not provide adaptive responses.

The process of development, as opposed to the general process of evolution, can be thought of as that process of change which reduces a population's level of vulnerability to extinction stemming from its own internal organization and mode of adaptation, or from environmental changes, events, or conditions, or from the relationship of these two sources to each other. This means that development as a concept pertains only to evolutionary change that increases a sociocultural system's survival capacity. Again, it is necessary to caution that the process of sociocultural evolution does not assure development; rather, it provides the mechanisms that lead to change and, therefore, to the survival of adaptive systems. But it does not insure survival itself; it merely assures extinction if adaptive mechanisms fail.

In the long run, if human societies are to continue to evolve, and at the same time develop and therefore survive, they must continually revise and improve their defenses against vulnerability by expanding their understanding of the relationships between sociocultural systems, their environment, and the vulnerability implicit in that relationship. Above all, they must develop the capacity to anticipate the long-range effects of short-term solutions to adaptation problems and compensate for the new forms of vulnerability that arise out of technological and other sociocultural modes of adaptation.

Disasters and Development

To return to the subject of disasters and their relationship to development, the two processes are intimately related for several reasons. First, sociocultural evolution is a process by which a population evolves patterns that reduce its vulnerability to its environment and to its own internal organization. Each small adaptive problem can be thought of as potentially a kind of minidisaster that, by threatening the survival of some population members, threatens the population as a whole. For example, by developing a technology and social organization that results in producing a stable food supply, an organized population reduces its vulnerability to famine. By developing methods for the production of dwellings, the population protects itself against vulnerability to climatic conditions or other environmental hazards. For these reasons, we can think of all sociocultural evolution, or development, as a process by which vulnerability to natural hazards is reduced. Disasters, small and large, personal and social, are exactly what a sociocultural system evolves to prevent. Thus, in a sense, vulnerability to survival hazards furnishes the motive power and the selective mechanism that guide the development process.

Second, a disaster as a social event must be regarded as a process that involves a sociocultural system's failure to protect a population from vulnerability to its environment, or from an event that occurs because of the internal vulnerability built into its own technology, social organization, or ideology. Disasters are the result of vulnerability that lies beyond the developed adaptive capacity of a sociocultural system; or they are a result of that very system which is used to adapt to normal environmental conditions or normal internal operational problems. In reverse, it can be said that disasters are the result of unsolved adaptive problems or that they are evidence of a lack of adaptation, and therefore of development, with respect to certain conditions important to a population's survival.

In addition, there is a third critical issue. Disasters intervene in the development process as it pertains to other important adaptive problems, and they redirect, deflect, retard, and on rare occasions accelerate the development process. If it can be assumed that the ordinary development process is directed toward solving problems of vulnerability associated with more mundane matters such as improving food supply, housing, health care, education, industrial production, and public welfare and security, then disasters such as earthquakes, floods, hurricanes, droughts, and technological accidents represent sudden and disruptive events that require the expenditure of resources, human energy, and attention that would normally have gone into improving solutions to these other problems. In developing societies where sociocultural systems provide only a precarious adaptation to survival problems and leave the majority of a population vulnerable to malnutrition, health hazards, unsatisfactory housing conditions, and other results of poverty, a disaster may prove to be an intolerable burden that retards or even reverses the development process, making living conditions even worse (Bates and Peacock 1987). On the other hand, disasters may provide the impetus to developmental change, not only resulting in lowered disaster vulnerability, but also improvements in other conditions related to development. For these reasons, disasters cannot be separated from development.

A fourth relationship between disasters and development has already been alluded to. The technological systems as well as the forms of social organization and ideology that are inseparable aspects of sociocultural systems may actually be responsible for producing disasters, both natural and man-made. Actually, as has been seen, all disasters are, in one sense, man-made because they represent a sociocultural system's failure to provide protection against some form of vulnerability. But there are three other faces to this issue. First, the very system used to reduce one type of vulnerability may introduce another form. For example, houses protect against climatic conditions and reduce a population's vulnerability to health hazards stemming from such conditions. Houses may nevertheless be vulnerable to high-energy environmental events such as earthquakes, tornadoes, and hurricanes. When these structures collapse, they actually cause deaths and injuries (e.g., Bates and Killian 1981; Bates, Farrell, and Glittenberg 1979). Of course, such a disaster depends on the technology used in construction; nevertheless, houses that work well in reducing vulnerability to climate may actually produce vulnerability to other conditions, even to radon gas.

The second type of man-made disaster refers to the more indirect effects of a sociocultural system and is exemplified by that system's effects on its own environment and the feedback of these effects on the system itself. This form is illustrated by such phenomena as the pollution of the air and water supply of a population as a by-product of the technology it employs to solve other problems, or by changes in climate due to those phenomena that affect the sunlight reaching the earth or that result in acid rain (Brown 1990, 1991a, 1991b, and 1992; Flavin 1991; World Resources Institute 1990). Another example would be changes in patterns of rainfall because of deforestation or overgrazing (Durning and Brough 1992; Postel and Rayan 1991). In these cases the technology employed to solve one adaptive problem has the side effect of producing another, often more threatening, and difficult problem to solve.

Still a third type of man-made disaster stemming from the development process is the so-called technological accident that either directly threatens a population because of its immediate impact or because of its long-range effect on the environment. One class of such events involves the uncontrolled, accidental release of poison gases or chemicals into the air or water supply, or of radiation from accidents at atomic power plants, or the occurrence of violent explosions, airplane crashes, or train wrecks in populated areas. A second subtype involves accidents such as oil spills, improper toxic waste disposal, or contaminants in the food supply resulting from substances used in food production.

All of these disasters are outcomes of a development process whose evolution took place as a means of adapting a population to other forms of uncertainty and vulnerability. They, too, testify to the inseparable nature of development and disasters. Development is oriented by the very nature of the human adaptive process at reducing vulnerability to disasters, but at the same time this process results in trade-offs among forms of vulnerability.

Disasters and development are intimately interrelated in one final way. Every sociocultural system employs three types of cultural mechanisms to adapt a population to itself and to its environment: (1) a technological system, (2) forms of social organization, and (3) an ideological system. Each one of these aspects of culture reduces certain types of vulnerability and at the same time exposes a population to other forms. Enough has already been said about technology. Suffice it to add that every society, no matter how primitive, employs a technology, and that technology reduces some form of vulnerability, but at the same time leaves the population open to other forms, some caused by the technology's internal nature.

Social organization is also an aspect of every sociocultural system. It refers to modes of organizing a human population according to a division of labor in order to develop and use a technological system or to pursue activities mandated by an ideological system. Every form of social organization creates a set of interdependencies among the specialized parts of a social system. It also yields a population's collective adaptation to an environment. The introduction of a division of labor as a means of organization provides a set of mechanisms for protecting a population against vulnerability. Some forms of social organization may increase production of the things needed for survival, and they may raise the probability that a population will increase its level of adaptation. Those forms may also increase the probability of further technological development, or increase the effectiveness of its use. In a broad sense, socioeconomic systems such as feudalism, capitalism, or socialism, as well as earlier systems based on hunting-gathering, horticulture, or agriculture, represent not only technological and ideological systems but forms of social organization that incorporate complex webs of human association into a collective means of reducing vulnerability by providing solutions to adaptive problems (Lenski 1966; Lenski, Lenski, and Nolan 1991).

Each such system is vulnerable to disruption stemming from its own internal order. Thus, famines, economic depressions, resource shortages, and even plagues are related to the form that these systems take. It is probably also true that the capacity to generate new adaptive solutions to old or to emerging vulnerabilities is closely related to how such systems are organized. Certainly a whole society's vulnerability to disruption by internal causes seems to increase as its structure becomes more complex and interdependent. For example, modern industrial societies are extremely vulnerable to disruption of their energy supply or of the complex communications and transportation systems upon which they depend. Since these societies are themselves interdependent and technologically advanced, they provide the most affluent forms of adaptation and are the most vulnerable to sudden and complete collapse, should their energy supply be cut off or their communications and transportation systems fail.

Ideology also plays an important role in relation to both disasters and development. It can be defined as that aspect of culture which includes beliefs and values as well as language and other symbolic codes, and it supplies its users with a worldview that incorporates a set of explanations for both natural and social phenomena (Lenski, Lenski, and Nolan 1991). This latter aspect of ideology contains a view of how the world works, and in modern industrial societies it would include both science and religion as well as the folklore used to explain events such as earthquakes, droughts, floods, and other catastrophes that are part of the experience of the population sharing the ideology.

It is apparent that ideology profoundly affects the types of adaptive patterns that a population employs. For example, a belief system that explains disasters in supernatural terms will foster magical or religious adaptive patterns. If the gods cause earthquakes when they are angry, the solution is to placate the gods. If disease is caused by magic spells cast by enemies, then the protection against disease is magical. Such a belief system will foster the development of religious or magical technologies but not necessarily a physical technology or a change in social organization that reduces vulnerability. Perhaps not so obvious to the industrialized West is the fact that a materialistic value system, which explains everything in scientific terms, favors engineering solutions to problems of vulnerability and acts as if there is a potential physical technology to meet every need and solve every adaptation problem. This includes vulnerability to such major natural forces as earthquakes, floods, and hurricanes. The strategy is to attack nature and transform it if possible, and if not, to build strong technological defenses against it. Thus, to prevent floods, dams are constructed, streams are channeled, levies are built, and bridges and other structures are made strong enough to withstand the force of floodwaters. Earthquakes may also be conceived of as being conquerable by engineering human structures to withstand them.

The point that may be missed by those devoted to this view is that such solutions (1) require enormous investments and divert resources away from use in reducing other vulnerabilities. Other possible solutions such as removing the population from exposed areas, thus reorganizing the spatial distribution of the activities carried on within a society, may considerably reduce the costs of reducing vulnerability. (2) Such solutions create new forms of vulnerability by exposing a population to a new threat, for example, the 100-year flood in which a system of dams and levies fails, or an earthquake of a magnitude beyond that engineered for. There are also environmental impacts associated with such technological solutions that may have feedback effects, producing new, unanticipated vulnerabilities.

In addition, ideologies may favor value systems that emphasize matters which are not directly related to survival but which encourage the use of resources to satisfy socially created wants. For example, a materialistic ideology that places high value on the accumulation of property and the demonstration of social worth through affluence encourages the profligate use of resources to meet demands that do not improve the survival capacity of a population but, in the long run, result in high negative impacts on the environment. Such a value system may explain poverty as evidence of unfitness for survival and wealth as a demonstration of superior qualities, thus justifying the continuous vulnerability of a segment of a human population to conditions threatening its survival. This point makes it apparent that ideology has the capacity to divert the evolutionary process by which human populations attempt to improve their survival capacity toward goals and objectives that, in the long run, have negative effects.

This discussion suffices to make the point that disasters and development are so closely related that one cannot be understood without the other. Every developmental change has implications for disaster vulnerability. Similarly, every disaster and every disaster response have significance for the development process. While this point is most easily perceived in the context of developing societies, it is also the case in the most economically and technologically advanced ones.

Especially true is the fact that the intimate relationship between disasters and development has significance for technological transfers from one society to another. It is here that the close relationship between technology, social organization, and ideology is of greatest importance to understanding development as a process, and disaster mitigation as a part of that process. Although technological solutions to problems of vulnerability may be available in the "developed world," such solutions may be inappropriate, indeed impossible, in a lesser-developed context where they do not fit the ideological system or the social organization and where they may create greater vulnerability to other threats to the population to which they are transferred.

It is time now to consider a second aspect of the theoretical problem of associating disasters with development. Not only do societies differ in vulnerability to their environment, and thus to disasters; but within societies, individual social units such as households differ. It is necessary therefore to conceptualize a process through which households and, in the long run, other parts of society provide themselves with the means to adapt to their environment within the context of a given society. At the same time, it is necessary to think through the relationship of a household's adaptation to disaster vulnerability. This exercise will result in a theoretical foundation for using a cost-weighting approach in creating the Domestic Assets Scale.

The Household-Level Adaptive Process

In order to establish themselves as social and economic units, households (defined as a group of people who share a common dwelling unit) go through a process of accumulating a store of capital equipment that they use to perform normal household functions. This accumulation process involves investing economic resources and human labor in acquiring the physical objects that constitute the household's living conditions. For purposes of this study, these physical items will be referred to as domestic assets. Thus, a cooking stove is a domestic asset; a housing unit is a domestic asset; so are refrigerators, bathtubs and toilets, beds, dining room tables, electric lights, etc. Also, in poorer households more primitive items are domestic assets: for example, a dishpan, a washtub, a wood-burning stove, an outdoor privy.

From the perspective discussed above, these domestic assets are the devices that the household group employs to adapt to its environment, providing the tools needed for the group to survive as a social unit. In this sense, the technological systems employed by the household are the devices that reduce vulnerability to the physical and sociocultural environment in which the group functions as a social unit.

A normal process exists by which households in any society accumulate domestic assets. The collection of domestic assets represents the *domestic capital* that the household controls and uses. It can be thought of as a set of capital resources employed to produce goods and services used in the household in much the same way as a manufacturing firm's capital resources are viewed to be the means by which it produces its output.

The accumulation of domestic assets requires investment of money or human labor. As a consequence, each asset has an economic value that could be computed in terms of the amount of human labor needed to acquire it or in terms of what it would cost if bought on the market. In either case, it is possible to conceive of the total investment that a household has made, at any point, in the domestic assets it employs. This total value would represent the cost of establishing or reestablishing a set of living conditions that themselves represent a household's level of adaptation to a set of environmental conditions. These conditions include both the natural and the sociocultural environment in which the household is embedded.

The process of a society's economic development always involves an increasingly greater accumulation of capital assets both for households and for economic enterprises such as manufacturing firms. Thus, as households develop economically, they accumulate domestic assets that cost more and therefore require a larger investment. The total cost of a household's domestic assets will be greatest when capital-intensive rather than labor-intensive technologies are employed. These things will hold true across societies as well as among economic strata within the same society. Also, as a household in a given society advances economically within its own economy, it will normally acquire domestic assets that have an increasingly higher economic value. As a consequence, it can be expected that as the per capita GNP of a country increases, this increase will be reflected in the total value of domestic assets associated with the median household in that country.

Also, the degree of economic inequality in a society can be measured by the characteristics of the distribution of domestic assets for households. In a society with a high level of inequality, a few households will have a very large monetary investment in domestic assets, while the great majority of households will have only small monetary investments in the technology they employ to perform domestic functions.

Disasters destroy and damage domestic assets, which has the effect of producing what can be called *deaccumulation* since the value of domestic assets is reduced. In other words, disasters cause a *negative economic accumulation process*. In extreme cases, the value of a household's assets is reduced to zero. Thus, a *reaccumulation* process is required. That is, a new set of investments must be made for the household to resume normal activities. The recovery process can be monitored through each stage by examining the household's store of domestic assets at various points in time after a disaster has produced deaccumulation (e.g., Bates 1982; Bates and Peacock 1987, 1989; Peacock, Killian, and Bates 1987; Rodeheaver 1990).

One important set of questions requiring research involves the determinants of the normal pre-disaster accumulation process. Another set asks whether the disaster recovery process brings about a distortion or change in the reaccumulation process. Does the introduction of recovery programs into disaster situations change the process by which households accumulate assets in such a way that the distribution of these assets in the affected community or society is changed? Or, putting it differently: To what extent do normal as opposed to disaster-related processes affect the accumulation of domestic assets following disasters? Do certain types of reconstruction programs accelerate or retard reaccumulation? Do they unequally affect households from different social classes, from different types of communities, from different ethnic groups? How are different types of households affected? Do female-headed households fare as well as male-headed households? Do young households do as well or better than older ones?

All of these questions can be researched if the value and type of the domestic assets associated with a household can be measured, especially if the measurements can be done at different points in time. To do so, it is necessary to understand that the processes of accumulation, deaccumulation, and reaccumulation are all part of a general process related to general social and economic development. Disasters are merely a special case in the same process that involves the economic development of a household and of the society or community in which it is located.

Disasters inevitably affect the development process since they require resources to be invested in the reaccumulation of capital rather than in the continuation of the normal accumulation process. If these resources are drawn completely from within the affected community, the required reconstruction process will divert resources from normal developmental processes and retard those processes for the community as a whole. At the same time, it is possible that these resources will come from outside the community that is affected by the disaster, but still from within the society, in which case the affected community's development may be only temporarily retarded. If resources are disproportionate to loss, representing an increase over normal investment, the community may actually accelerate its development. Even so, normal development processes in the total society will be retarded in proportion to the cost of reaccumulation if no foreign aid is used (Bates and Peacock 1987). The same sort of reasoning applies in the case of foreign aid. With foreign aid, investments will have whatever retarding effect they produce in the donor countries, while they may actually produce a net positive effect on investment in capital resources in the country affected by a disaster.

The point is that disasters affect the social and economic development process by producing deaccumulation of capital resources and by introducing disaster aid to support the reaccumulation process. Disasters have the potential to change the distribution and type of resources employed to support normal activities and can represent either a threat to development or an opportunity for positive change. The measurement of household living conditions using a domestic assets approach therefore supplies a means of monitoring one aspect of development at the household level. By doing so, it supplies a means of measuring normal accumulation processes, as well as the deaccumulation and reaccumulation processes associated with disasters (Rodeheaver 1990). A domestic assets scale, such as the one being developed here, furnishes a measure useful in evaluating the impact of development programs on household living conditions. In the same way, it furnishes a measure by which disaster reconstruction programs can be evaluated in terms of their effectiveness in restoring household living conditions.

Human societies develop by providing solutions to adaptation problems in the form of sociocultural systems and subsystems. These systems evolve as people attempt to adapt to their environment by developing means of reducing their vulnerability to environmental conditions and to conditions that arise within the population itself. One part of the development process is concerned with creating the technological means of lowering vulnerability by increasing the probability that vital functions will be performed on a regularized basis. This form of technological evolution involves inventing or introducing technological systems into the sociocultural system as people learn to cope with their environment and their survival problems relative to it. The development process also involves the actual production, distribution, and accumulation of the capital resources represented by this technology. At the community level, this accumulation process is concerned with actually producing the infrastructural resources that the community employs to carry out its various adaptive functions—for example, the actual building of roads and highways, water and power systems, schools, churches, hospitals, factories, and commercial establishments. At the household level, the process involves building housing units and accumulating the domestic capital employed to carry on household functions.

Disasters intervene in this development process, not only by threatening human lives and physical well-being, but by damaging and destroying part or all of the physical capital that has been accumulated to allow people to solve various adaptive problems or to perform functions important to their survival as well as satisfying the values embedded in their ideological system. This impact on the accumulated capital resources of the community, or of households, affects the development process. It requires reinvestment in the accumulation of capital resources and creates a situation in which the normal development process may be deflected, retarded, reversed, or accelerated, depending on the manner in which the reconstruction process is carried out (Bates et al. 1963).

The normal accumulation process can be monitored if a measure can be devised that accurately assesses changes in the living conditions of households in terms of the physical capital used to perform normal household functions. Likewise, the impact of disasters can be measured and the process of deaccumulation monitored by use of the same method.

Use of a domestic assets approach promises to allow the study of the relationship among the technological systems employed by a household and the vulnerability of households to various man-made and natural hazards since this approach provides a criterion variable that can be associated in research with other measures of these hazards. It also provides a tool through which the effects of both development and disaster reconstruction programs can be evaluated in terms of their effects on living conditions. This evaluation can be accomplished by using the Domestic Assets Scale as a dependent variable in studies that measure other variables associated with development and reconstruction program characteristics. Thus, the Domestic Assets Scale is a general research instrument useful in measuring both disasters and development. Its utility, however, depends on its cross-cultural validity and a clear understanding of its relationship to both disasters and development.

Chapter 2

General Methodology

The objective of this research is to develop a cross-cultural scale for measuring the impact of disasters on households that will also be useful in measuring household socioeconomic status and for monitoring the recovery process following disasters. At the outset, it was assumed that the scale being created should also be capable of measuring the dimension of social and economic development called the process of domestic capital accumulation (chapter 1). Recognition of these requirements grew out of experience in dealing with problems associated with evaluating the effects of reconstruction programs on households in a study of the 1976 Guatemalan earthquake (Bates 1982; Bates, Killian, and Peacock 1984; Peacock, Killian, and Bates 1987).

In studying the recovery process following a disaster, a technique is needed to measure the impact of a physical disaster agent on households, and also to measure the effects of reconstruction efforts on restoring living conditions damaged or destroyed in the disaster. As already pointed out, disasters have an impact on the physical living conditions of households, damaging and destroying houses and their contents. Reconstruction programs are directed toward repairing and replacing the losses suffered in such events. Reconstruction research, therefore, requires that measures be developed to evaluate disaster losses at the household level and also to measure progress toward recovery. Such measures can serve as criteria against which to evaluate reconstruction programs. They can also serve as the basis for studying the relationships between household socioeconomic variables and disaster losses, and therefore, as a basis for examining the relationship between disaster vulnerability and household characteristics.

To measure disaster losses, it is necessary to be able to measure a household's pre-disaster situation, since losses must always be evaluated against pre-disaster conditions. The requirement, therefore, is for an instrument or scale that can assess the same variable or set of variables at several points in time, using the same internal logic and metric. In the Guatemalan Earthquake Study, the Domestic Assets Scale was created for this purpose (Bates 1982; Killian and Bates 1982; Bates, Killian, and Peacock 1984; Peacock, Killian, and Bates 1987; Rodeheaver 1990). It followed the logic given in chapter 1 and was used to measure the level of domestic assets associated with a household at several points in time:

1. The level of domestic assets of individual households the day before the disaster.
2. The level of domestic assets of the same households the day after the disaster, when damage and loss had reduced their value or completely destroyed it.
3. The level of domestic assets for the same households at intervals after the reconstruction process had been introduced to restore the pre-disaster situation.

The scale used the same set of domestic assets items to obtain all of these measures in a longitudinal research design, which also employed the same scale to measure the domestic assets of households in a control group that had not suffered earthquake losses. The objective in Guatemala was to monitor the normal process through which households accumulate domestic assets, and to compare it to the recovery or re-accumulation process taking place in communities within the disaster zone, thereby assessing the effects of the disaster on normal accumulation processes.

This sort of research design requires a measuring instrument that is useful in studying the development process as it applies to households in both disaster and nondisaster situations. To do so, a theoretical foundation is required that justifies the instrument's use by relating it conceptually both to disasters and development (see discussion in chapter 1).

The Domestic Assets Scale used in Guatemala was tailored to fit the Guatemalan case, and it worked reasonably well as a criterion variable for use in monitoring recovery (Bates 1982; Bates, Killian, and Peacock 1984; Peacock, Killian, and Bates 1987; Bates and Peacock 1987). The current study attempts to expand this technique's use to other cultures by conducting a more rigorous methodological test and by revising the instrument in such ways as to make it more valid cross-culturally. The study is also directed toward solving problems associated with the use of monetary weights to achieve cross-cultural comparability, when it is known that exchange rates for various currencies fluctuate greatly through time and, in any case, are poor measures of the actual relative purchasing power of money.

Methodological Problems Requiring Solutions

To achieve the goals of this research, several methodological and theoretical problems had to be solved. These problems had been dealt with only tentatively in the Guatemalan case, and better solutions were needed. The critical problems requiring solutions were these:

1. It was necessary to select a broader and better defined set of household functions on which to base the development of the domestic assets items.
2. For each functional area it was necessary to compile a completely exhaustive inventory of technological items used anywhere in the world to perform that function. For example, a list of every conceivable type of cooking stove or heat source for cooking had to be assembled to create the interview item related to food preparation.
3. A means had to be devised for determining the monetary value of each domestic assets item so that cost weights could be assigned within each sample community. For example, a way of obtaining the cost of each type of cooking stove had to be devised.
4. Because each country employs a different currency, and exchange rates are unreliable, a method of converting cost figures into an international monetary unit based on the actual relative value of domestic assets had to be worked out.
5. A research design for field-testing the international instrument under cross-cultural conditions had to be developed, and an actual field test had to be conducted in countries that differed in culture and levels of development.
6. Data obtained in different languages in different cultural settings separated by long distances had to be processed, analyzed, and interpreted in such ways as to assess the method's utility and validity.
7. To accomplish all of these things, an international research team had to be assembled and organized in such a way as to bring to bear the talents and cultural perspectives of team members on developing a common, relatively large research effort.

Subsequent chapters will deal in detail with items 1 through 4; the rest of this chapter will be devoted to describing the general strategy used to solve these problems. More detailed methodological issues will be discussed in later chapters. We will begin with the research team and its organization.

The Research Team and Sample of Countries

In light of its critical importance to the methodology of this research, the research team's characteristics and organization need to be known and understood. Cross-cultural research requires cross-cultural thinking and collaboration. Bringing together researchers from various societies with different cultural and professional backgrounds to design a common measuring instrument is an important part of the cross-cultural research process since it significantly affects the research process and outcome.

In addition to the principal investigator and two Ph.D.-level research assistants from the University of Georgia, all of whom are sociologists, the international research team consisted of (1) Carlos Aramburu, anthropologist, Andean Institute, Lima, Peru; (2) Manuel Esparza, anthropologist, Institute of History and Anthropology, Oaxaca, Mexico; (3) Aydin Germen, city planner, retired Professor of City Planning, University of Ankara, Turkey; (4) Dennis Mileti, sociologist, Colorado State University, United States; (5) Josip Obradovic, sociologist, University of Zagreb, Yugoslavia; and (6) Carlo Pelanda, sociologist, Institute of International Sociology, Gorizia, Italy.

The countries represented by this team were selected because they represent different levels of economic and technological development as measured by World Bank figures on GNP per capita, energy consumption, etc., and they range from near the top to the lower middle of the scale represented by these measures. The countries were also selected because they more or less regularly experience violent earthquakes, and therefore the possibility of a disaster occurring in one of them during the term of the study could be used to field-test damage estimation techniques. Finally, they were selected because in each one scholars could be found who were fluent in English, were aware of the importance of disasters and disaster reconstruction because of personal familiarity with such events, and were interested in collaborating on research that would improve our understanding of the sociocultural impact of such events and possibly improve our ability to evaluate reconstruction programs. Unfortunately, because of funding constraints, countries from the lower range of the GNP per capita scale and from Asian and African cultural areas were not included. It is our hope that future research using the methods and procedures detailed in this study will be undertaken to establish the utility of this approach in these areas. Nevertheless, the sample countries included in this study do offer a relatively wide range of economic and cultural differences with which to assess the utility of the domestic assets approach.

To solve the various problems listed above, the team met as a group at three week-long workshop sessions held at the University of Georgia, during which intensive discussions were held concerning each of the methodological and theoretical issues to be faced. In addition, the project's principal investigator visited each country, sometimes on several occasions, to work out particular problems and to communicate information concerning progress and ideas for improvement of the work coming from other team participants. Meanwhile, telephone and mail contacts were frequently used to coordinate activities.

The team's first two meetings were devoted to developing the research methodology and to designing a common survey instrument containing the Domestic Assets Scale and the necessary background information and validation items to test that scale. At these meetings the general theoretical basis of the scale was discussed and debated, especially its strengths and weaknesses for cross-cultural research. In addition, a preliminary version of an interview schedule, prepared by the Georgia research group based on its Guatemalan experience, was used as a basis for discussions and for designing new domestic assets items and items planned for use in validating the scale. By this group process a set of functional areas for developing domestic assets items was agreed on, and the actual items for use in obtaining data were developed.

The typical problem was to design questions and response categories that would work in all six countries and that would include every known type of physical equipment or facility used to perform a given function. For example, it was necessary to compile a list of different types of stoves or cooking arrangements used in any society known to the research team so that a response category representing each one could be provided on the interview schedule. After these decisions were reached, it was necessary to work out descriptions of each item so that it could be recognized in each country and coded in the same way by different interviewers. In other words, the group had to decide what was meant by such terms as fireplace, charcoal grill, hibachi, hot plate, gas stove, and other alternative forms of domestic assets used for cooking. Furthermore, because the plan was to cost-weight these items, and because the design and cost of many such items vary within and between societies, the team had to agree on subcategories within items. For example, for electric stoves, size and design categories were established and described in detail so that comparable data could be obtained and cost figures could be applied to more or less identical domestic assets items in each country. One category consisted of large electric stoves with two self-cleaning ovens; another category of electric stoves with a single non-self-cleaning oven designed for small apartments.

Once all of the items had been developed and defined, a computer coding system that would be consistent across countries had to be worked out, and a format for the research instrument had to be developed. The plan was to have the English version of the interview schedule translated into the appropriate languages for each country, but to preserve the same format and numerical coding system so that interviews in various languages could be entered into computer files that were exactly the same for each country, and also so that they could be entered into files by an English-speaking data processor if necessary. This was important because computer resources and data processing personnel were not available in all countries. In the long run, the Italian and Yugoslav data were entered into computer files in Italy and Yugoslavia. The data from Peru, Mexico, Turkey, and the United States were processed in Georgia where Spanish-speaking data analysts were available. The Turkish data were carefully entered on code sheets by the Turkish collaborator after reviewing and correcting problems stemming from interviewer errors or comments written on the interview schedules.

The field surveys were directed by the collaborating scholars from each country using a team of local interviewers assembled and trained by him. Each collaborator also translated the interview schedule, managed its duplication, and oversaw the quality control process, checking interviews for completeness and accuracy and correcting problems of inconsistency.

Sampling Plan

This study's research design called for testing the domestic assets technique by conducting a sample survey in each of the six participating countries. Our plan was to select a community in each country and to interview a random sample of households to determine whether the interview schedule provided all of the possible response categories needed to apply the domestic assets technique in each cultural setting; we also wanted to determine whether the scale actually measures differences in socioeconomic status among households in each culture by comparing it with other validating measures thought to measure related variables. Accordingly, the research team selected a city in each country as a test site.

Cities were chosen to be roughly comparable in terms of their place in each country's political economy. All were medium-size provincial cities that included some light industry and households ranging from poor to relatively rich in relative terms within the country's economy. These cities cannot be thought of as being representative of their countries; therefore, comparisons between them must be restricted to the cities themselves. They should be thought of as cities that exist within the context of the political economy and culture of countries which differ in their level of economic development. Particular cities, however, may fall above or below the average level of economic affluence for the country as a whole. This is particularly the case with the U.S. sample, which, because of the requirement that the study be done in an earthquake-prone area, was conducted in Santa Barbara, California, a relatively well-to-do city in an affluent state. The Italian city, Udine, is undoubtedly more economically developed than cities of comparable size in southern Italy; therefore, it is probably above the national average in possessing domestic assets. The Mexican city, Oaxaca, is located in a relatively poor region of Mexico, although it is the most economically developed center in that region. Söke, the Turkish research site, is located in an agricultural region that specializes in cotton production and is probably somewhat better off economically than other cities of comparable size, but lower in standing than large urban centers such as Istanbul, Ismir, or Ankara. Chosica, the research site in Peru, is northeast of Lima and is a small transportation center and a resort area used by the urban dwellers of Lima. It contains neither the extremes of wealth or of poverty found in Lima. Slavonski Brod, the Yugoslav city studied, is a medium-size community between Zagreb and Belgrade. It contains a number of light industries and is located in one of Yugoslavia's best agricultural regions. This region and city are better off economically than other Yugoslav regions such as Macedonia, Bosnia, and Montenegro. It is probably near the average for similar-size cities in Serbia and Croatia, and probably lower in general economic status than similar areas in Slovenia. In all likelihood it slightly overestimates the distribution of domestic assets for the country as a whole.

In each city a random sample of households was interviewed using a stratified area sampling method. Each city was divided into high, medium, and low socioeconomic sectors of roughly equal size. A sample of areas was randomly drawn to be proportionately representative of the number of areas falling within each category. Then a sample of households was drawn from these areas using a standard sampling interval. In case a stratum yielded less than 30 interviews, it was oversampled to raise the number of cases to 30. When data were analyzed, the samples were weighted to correct for oversampling or undersampling. Because of differences in the cost of interviewing, and because of limited funds, sample sizes varied from one country to another, so that the sampling fraction differs from one case to another, but the representation of high, medium, and low socioeconomic groups has been held constant for all samples so that statistics such as means and medians can be compared. The numbers of interviews conducted in each city is given in table 2.1.

The Problem of Cost-Weighting

The Domestic Assets Scale uses monetary weights to furnish the metric used in achieving a household's domestic assets score. This strategy, as noted in chapter 1, was chosen because it has several advantages over the type of scoring used on standard level of living scales and also over the technical efficiency method used by Belcher.

One of this approach's main advantages is that it is easy to interpret the

Table 2.1. Sample Areas and Sample Sizes

City and Country	Size (N)
Santa Barbara, California, United States	239
Udine, Italy	230
Slavonski Brod, Yugoslavia	302
Oaxaca, Mexico	350
Söke, Turkey	370
Chosica, Peru	352

meaning of the total score for a household since it corresponds to the total market value or replacement cost of the set of household domestic assets items employed in the scale. It therefore can be interpreted as equivalent to the monetary investment represented by the household's living conditions. In the case of a disaster that destroys all of a household's domestic assets, it can be thought of as the amount of financial loss suffered, or more correctly as the cost of replacing those lost assets if they were restored exactly as they were and no inflationary price changes occurred as a result of the disaster. Even if inflation does occur, by using an estimate of the inflation rate, replacement costs can be recalculated to take price increases into account.

By using the theory of development discussed in chapter 1 and the concepts of accumulation, deaccumulation, and reaccumulation, a cost-weighted Domestic Assets Scale can be associated with a theory of disasters and development. The assumption is that higher levels of economic and technological development involve increasing investments in domestic assets to achieve less vulnerability to environmental hazards and to hazards that threaten the health and well-being of household members. Therefore, differences in the median level of domestic assets among countries can serve as an indicator of differences in levels of development among those countries. This is justified by the fact that the most primitive living conditions found in the poorest households in the least-developed societies employ domestic assets that have small monetary values and require small economic investments, while the assets employed in the most technologically advanced societies require large economic investments.

It is quite possible that highly developed and least-developed societies differ far less in the relative amount of human labor represented by those investments than in the monetary value associated with them. For example, if a country's median wage were used to calculate the number of hours of work represented by the monetary value of that country's median level of domestic assets, it is conceivable that countries would converge. This sort of manipulation is made possible by using monetary weights to scale living conditions, adding another advantage to this strategy's use.

Another advantage is that cost-weighting yields a score that reflects a household's relative economic standing within the context of its own country's political economy. Poor households have smaller investments in domestic assets than richer ones. As a consequence, domestic assets scores can be used to measure economic standing, and their use in connection with the same households over time can be used to measure changes in socioeconomic status. Like any measure that assesses some dimension of wealth or income, cost-weighting can be used to measure inequality and, therefore, changes in inequality as they relate to development processes and programs or to disaster assistance efforts.

The final and perhaps the methodologically most important advantage of cost-weighting is that it is also self-weighting. Housing, which is more costly than cooking or clothes washing equipment, is given a weight proportional to its monetary value, as are all items included in the scale. The same is true when a technique for measuring loss is applied to the same figures. The loss of a dwelling unit is given greater weight than the loss of a stove or refrigerator. Furthermore, this approach applies across cultural settings, social classes, and levels of development. That is, in poor households in underdeveloped societies, the self-weighting system operates in the same manner as it does in richer, more highly developed ones. It also can be applied between countries if a solution to the exchange rate problem can be found.

The Price Survey

To obtain the information needed to cost-weight domestic assets items in each country, a price survey instrument was designed, and data were obtained from a market survey in each research setting. This price survey listed every domestic assets item encountered in the survey in each country and supplied a definition of these items so that data could be obtained from suppliers. Items that were self-constructed or could not be found on the market were given an arbitrary weight equivalent to $1.00. This applied to such things as crude fireplaces constructed of loose stones, or salvaged wooden boxes used to store food. The survey obtained a high, medium, and low price for each item where prices varied, and the monetary weight assigned to the item for the scale in that country was the value halfway between the two extremes. All prices were obtained in local currencies, and the exchange rate at the time between that currency and U.S. dollars was recorded so that conversions could be made.

Because of limited funding, no attempt was made to obtain prices from every source of supply in the community. Only those suppliers who were considered average or usual sources for each kind of item were surveyed. In Italy and the United States, where such national distributors as Sears and Roebuck, J. C. Penney, and Badcock distribute catalogs listing prices, these prices were used on the assumption that these items were available nationally at fixed prices. Here, again, the price used was halfway between the high and low price for a given kind of item.

Once these prices were obtained, they were associated by a computer program with each domestic assets item for each household. Thus, the price obtained from the market survey in each country for a large electric stove with two self-cleaning ovens was assigned to every household in that country which had such a stove. The same procedure was followed for every domestic assets item in each country so that in the end the value of the domestic assets of a household could be obtained by adding together all of their cost weights. This resulted in a domestic assets score stated in local currency.

Currency Conversion into
a Common Monetary Unit

The use of the Domestic Assets Scale in comparative studies of a cross-cultural nature depends on the researchers' ability to convert different monetary units into a common currency. For example, there must be some method of converting domestic assets scores stated in Italian lira or Yugoslav dinars into U.S. dollars or Mexican pesos. The simplest solution is to use bank exchange rates, but such rates may fluctuate rapidly and are known to be relatively poor measures of actual purchasing power. Since this study was undertaken in 1984, the exchange rates between U.S. dollars, Mexican pesos, Peruvian soles, and Yugoslav dinars have changed radically, sometimes as much as 1,000 percent. If one were to compare a household in Santa Barbara having a certain combination of domestic assets with a household in Lima or Zagreb that has the same domestic assets in, say, 1984 and 1989, the same assets in Yugoslavia and Peru would appear to have radically lost value relative to those in California, when in fact nothing at all had changed except for the exchange rate. A given domestic assets item—for example, a refrigerator—does not gain or lose *use* value as its price stated in inflated currency values changes.

The living conditions represented by a given combination of domestic assets should be thought of as representing the same level of living conditions, no matter how widely exchange rates fluctuate and no matter how much inflation goes on within a country as the fluctuation occurs. For cross-cultural research purposes, households in two different countries that have the same assets should be given the same domestic assets score when the two currencies are converted into a common monetary unit. Also, domestic assets scores between countries should not be allowed to fluctuate according to changes in exchange rates, which are influenced by political decisions that tend to favor the currencies of the most economically powerful nations, or by inflationary price changes. If two households have the same domestic assets in Time 2 that they had in Time 1, their scores should remain the same when compared cross-culturally and longitudinally.

To overcome some of these problems, the World Bank, for example, uses exchange rates based on a three-year period rather than those for a single year, and researchers often use consumer price indexes to control for inflationary price alterations. In this study we will employ two procedures to convert national currencies. Chapter 5 will deal more completely with how conversions were undertaken, but the general logic employed in their development can be discussed here.

The first conversion method was to simply utilize exchange rates in effect during the data collection period to convert national currencies into U.S. dollars. In light of the rapid fluctuations that often occurred, as in Peru and Yugoslavia, average rates were calculated over three to six months. These averages were then used in converting to U.S. dollars. This method, however, in light of the above discussion is clearly less than satisfactory.

To achieve comparability across sample communities, a technique similar to the purchasing power parity method employed by Kravis, Heston, and Summers (1978a, 1978b, 1982) in their work for the United Nations was employed (see also Summers and Heston 1984, 1988; Summers, Kravis, and Heston 1980). In essence, this method uses a set of price figures for a standard market basket of products in different countries to arrive at a conversion rate stated in monetary units. For example, suppose a set of price figures could be obtained for a list of 100 common consumer items in two countries, each stated in its own currency. A ratio can then be obtained between the prices of each item in each country. Thus, the price of a certain type of kitchen stove is obtained for the United States and for Italy. In the United States the stove costs $500; in Italy it costs 700,000 lira. So the ratio is 700,000 to 500, or 1,400 to 1.

By following the same procedure, 100 ratios can be obtained and then employed to compute an average conversion ratio. This average, or mean, ratio can be used as a conversion rate to state the cost of the total market basket in a common currency. The same basket would then be equal to the same total value in each country.

There is the further possibility of computing weighted averages that allows high-cost items and/or items that are purchased at higher relative proportions to affect the mean price ratio more than lower-cost items. This technique uses the price ratio for a common set of products as the basis for arriving at a figure that can be used to convert one currency into another. It reflects the actual purchasing power of a currency rather than the international exchange rate, which is more dependent on money markets and international political factors than on domestic market conditions for products paid for in local currency. For this reason, we chose this method to convert domestic assets figures into a common monetary unit. (More will be said about this method in chapter 5, where actual figures based on the price surveys for domestic assets items in the six countries under investigation will be presented.)

Damage and Loss Estimation

The strategy for using the Domestic Assets Scale in a disaster is as follows. First, information is obtained on the domestic assets of a household just before the disaster occurred by using retrospective interview questions. Then an estimate of the amount of damage to each asset is obtained. This estimate is used to depreciate the asset's monetary value according to how much damage occurred. When this procedure is completed, a postdisaster domestic assets score results from adding together the depreciated values of the individual domestic assets items to obtain a total depreciated domestic assets score. This score is the value of a household's domestic assets immediately after disaster impact. By subtracting this score from the pre-disaster score, the amount of monetary loss, or deaccumulation, is computed. In turn, if so desired, this can be converted into a percentage loss.

In interview terms, respondents are first questioned concerning their predisaster living conditions. What kind of house did you live in at the time of the earthquake? What kind of stove did you have to cook your food on? How did you wash your clothes, etc.? Then they are asked a series of questions to establish what happened to each domestic asset in the disaster: for example, What happened to your house (apartment) in the earthquake? Using a set of probes, data is obtained on which a damage estimate can be based in terms of percentage loss. These loss categories are as follows:

1. Totally Destroyed   100 percent Loss
2. Heavy Damage   66 percent Loss
3. Light Damage   33 percent Loss
4. Undamaged   0 percent Loss

Each loss category is defined in terms of the item's use value under conditions of damage and a crude estimate of how much it would cost to repair it. For example, the destroyed category means that the item cannot be repaired but must be replaced. In the case of a house, it cannot be occupied again. The heavy damage category means that the item is totally unusable without extensive repairs costing more than half its original value. Light damage means the item can be used after minor repairs, and undamaged means that it can be used as is, even though it might have suffered slight cosmetic damage.

The aim of this procedure is to provide a simple damage estimate method that can be used by interviewers who are not expert insurance adjusters. Since many items are involved for each household, and since interviewers are expected to be on the disaster scene collecting these data within a short time after the event when the memories of victims are fresh, and since interviewers can visually inspect the household situation to improve accuracy, a reasonable estimate of differences in relative loss among households can be anticipated. Even though the damage categories are crude for each item and may overestimate or underestimate damage to particular items taken together, they are expected to yield results that estimate disaster impact reasonably well for individual households. This technique was employed in the Guatemalan Earthquake Study and proved useful there.

Validity and Reliability Assessment

Since this is a methodological study aimed at developing and pretesting a measuring instrument, a critical component will be assessing the reliability and validity of the Domestic Assets Scale. As a consequence, the data collected in each country included information intended for use in validating the measure. Most of this information was related to a household's socioeconomic status, including data on household income, education of household members, and expenditure patterns. The assumption is that the Domestic Assets Scale should correlate with other measures of socioeconomic status since it is intended to measure the monetary value of accumulated household property. In chapter 6 these data, along with other information, will be employed in a construct validation procedure (Zeller and Carmines 1980) to assess the domestic assets measure's validity.

Chapter 6 also will assess the reliability of the Domestic Assets Scale by examining, in detail, the measure's internal consistency. For example, the value of a household's dwelling unit—the technology that provides shelter—will be correlated against the value of other equipment and furnishings used in each of the remaining nine functional areas. The critical question will be whether the measure's components are performing in a consistent fashion; the greater the internal consistency, the more reliable the measure (Cronbach 1951; Carmines and Zeller 1979).

The unique nature of this project will be exploited throughout our assessment of the measure's validity and reliability. Often in the development of measuring instruments and scales, social scientists must wait for future studies to replicate their findings in order to gain additional confidence in the validity and reliability of their measures. This research differs by being designed to provide six independent replications of the same instrument within the context of a single project. As a result, each of the six community/country studies is treated as an independent replication of the same research design and instrument. Thus, the critical components of the validity and reliability analysis will be, first, an assessment using data from each sample site separately, and, second, an examination of the consistency in its performance across the six independent replications.

In addition, however, each country (and hence community) was selected to provide a range of sample sites that differ in levels of economic development and culture; the reason was to insure the measure's applicability when assessing living conditions in diverse economic and cultural settings. As a result, validity and reliability will also be assessed by combining the data into a single, all-encompassing set. Thus, rather than relying on some form of meta-analytic technique (Wolf 1986) to combine the sample-specific results, data from each sample are combined into a single set, allowing the measure's validity and reliability to be assessed over an extensive range of data. Combining six independent replications of the same research design and instrument will greatly strengthen the confidence with which this study can establish, or fail to establish, the utility of the domestic assets approach for measuring household living conditions cross-culturally.

Chapter 3

Description of the Sample Communities

The objective of this methodological study is to develop a cross-culturally useful scale for measuring disaster impact on individual households. To achieve this goal, it was necessary to field test the measuring instrument in a variety of cultural settings so that its cross-cultural utility could be assessed. It was also necessary to obtain information from field tests on additional forms of domestic assets that might be encountered in field situations, but which were not anticipated by the field instrument's designers. This was necessary because the finished instrument had to be standardized and precoded so that it could be used in any linguistic setting and nevertheless coded according to a standard numerical system that would make results obtained in one language immediately transformable into another. For example, an exhaustive list of types of cooking stoves had to be compiled and a code number assigned to each one. The field test was designed to discover unanticipated types of cooking stoves and other domestic assets and to allow an exhaustive coding system to be developed covering every possible response to each domestic assets question.

What was needed were sample sites in a set of countries representing different levels of economic development and different cultures. It was decided to select a single community within this set of nations that would meet household sampling objectives. The principal objective was to obtain data from households that varied in living conditions along a continuum from the very poor in a relatively underdeveloped country to the relatively rich in highly developed nations, and at the same time to have a reasonable sample within each country of variability among households from near the top to near the bottom of the socioeconomic ladder. Originally, ten countries were to be targeted for inclusion; however, because of funding limitations, four nations located in Africa and Asia were dropped from consideration. The remaining six countries chosen for study ranged from the lower middle to the high end of the continuum of GNP per capita. Within each nation a provincial city of moderate size, more or less conveniently located for research purposes, was selected, and a stratified random sample of households was interviewed to test the field instrument.

The sample communities needed to contain households falling into all socio-economic strata found in the country so that domestic assets items used by the very poor as well as the relatively rich would be encountered. The reasoning was that the actual domestic assets items used in households would differ by country and by social class within a country. Early on, it was decided that we did not need to overly concern ourselves with the extremely wealthy end of the continuum but would be satisfied with a sample that included moderately rich people who could afford the most expensive domestic assets, ruling out palatial homes as necessary to the study. Of more concern was inclusion of the extremes of poverty in the sample, so that variability in the domestic assets used by the very poor and the moderately poor could be measured.

While the data were collected in sample cities in each of six countries, it is important to emphasize that no one community can be truly representative of any nation. In fact, the cities used were not chosen for their representativeness. An attempt was made to select places that were roughly comparable within the political economies of their respective countries. This proved difficult since so many variables define the political economy of countries that themselves differ in levels of economic development and political organization. All that can be said about the comparability of the sample cities is that they are all of middle size (relative to the distribution of city sizes in their respective countries) and are all relatively provincial in that they are not at the core of the economic and political structures of their nations.

In this chapter the cities will be described so that the reader will be aware of the characteristics of the field test sites. The study's intention was not to measure socioeconomic differences among countries nor was it to arrive at a valid ranking of countries in terms of domestic assets. Rather, the objective was to develop a measuring instrument that could conceivably be used in this way if proper representative samples were drawn in the countries being compared. More to the point, the goal was to develop a scale that could measure disaster impacts in such a way that those impacts occurring in different communities, perhaps in different countries, could be compared. (To repeat, however: the selected sample sites are not meant to be representative of the countries in which they are located, and therefore the results obtained from them should not be used as a basis for comparing countries. On the other hand, since the samples drawn were carefully controlled to be representative, the cities themselves can be compared.) In the following pages, city descriptions prepared by the collaborating scholars in each country are presented as necessary background for understanding and interpreting the research results.

Chosica, Peru: Carlos E. Aramburu

Location

The city of Chosica is located in the district of Luringancho in Lima Province, 40 miles east of Lima, on the main road that connects the capital with the central Andes. Chosica is 800 meters above sea level and stretches for five kilometers upriver along the Lima–La Oroya Highway. The river Rimac, the main source of water and hydroelectric power for Lima, cuts Chosica in half. Toward the left bank, going from west to east, are the oldest sections and the main plaza.

Chosica became popular as a winter resort in the second half of the nineteenth century because of its pleasant climate, clean air, and relative proximity to Lima. Its average temperature is 24° centigrade in the daytime and 18° centigrade at night. Until the second decade of the twentieth century, the main access to the city was by train. By the 1930s a paved highway made road transportation the main form of travel.

In the 1950s and 1960s Chosica and its hinterland grew rapidly as a result of increasing migration from the central highlands. Since then, several shantytowns have developed, colonizing the dry lands that resulted from drainage areas formed by erosion from rains and landslides. These zones are considered hazardous because they are natural pathways of mud and water during the rainy season from January through March.

Population

The Luringancho district, of which Chosica is the main city, had 63,233 inhabitants according to the July 1981 census, with 11,581 dwellings. The central urban area of Chosica housed 52 percent of this population. Of these, 3 percent were under 15 years of age, almost 59 percent were between 15 and 64 years old, and the rest, 4 percent, were 65 or older. This age structure revealed a highly fertile population, with a large proportion living in poverty zones or shantytowns (*pueblos jovenes*). The illiteracy rate was about 10.4 percent among those over 15 years old. During the 1960s Chosica's urban population grew at the rate of 5.2 percent per year. In the 1970s growth slowed to 3.2 percent per year, and it was estimated at 2.6 percent per year for the 1980s.

Economic Activity

Chosica changed rapidly as an economic center in the late 1960s—after construction of the modern highway to Huancayo—of the central highlands. Several important industries were based there: paper mills, breweries, a shoe factory, and tile- and brick-making industries. The main hydroelectric plant serving Lima is located there. Also, numerous small restaurants and shops cropped up to cater to weekend visitors from the city. Several winter resorts or clubs owned by large companies and banks based in Lima are located in the city. Some 50 small chicken farms around Chosica supply local restaurants and markets in the capital. Agriculture's importance is diminishing as fertile land and water are claimed by urban expansion.

The total urban labor force was 18,919 by 1981. Unemployment was estimated at 7 percent. About one-third of the labor force worked in the service sector. Some 17 percent were employed in manufacturing, 14.4 percent in trade, restaurants, and hotels, most of them as petty street vendors. Ten percent were in the food industry (mainly chicken farms), and 7.6 percent in construction. Finally, about 6 percent worked in transportation and communications.

In relation to occupational status, the most recent census data showed that of 18,285 economically active individuals, 37 percent were blue-collar workers, 28 percent were white-collar workers, 23 percent were self-employed, 4 percent were domestic workers, 10 percent were employers, 1 percent were unpaid family labor, and 6 percent were nonspecified.

Housing and Services

Of the 11,581 dwellings in the Luringancho district of which Chosica had 6,791, the majority, or 87 percent, were detached houses or dwellings. For 53 percent of the dwellings, water services were by public connection to the house. More than 20 percent had a well, 11 percent had common faucets, 8 percent used running water from the river or open channel, 5 percent had tanks or water cylinders that were replenished by a water truck, and about 2.5 percent had one fountain within the communal building.

In-house sewage was present in 39 percent of the dwellings. Thirty percent had no sewage, and 19 percent had a pit or out-house. Finally, 72 percent of the homes had electricity, almost 15 percent used kerosene lamps, and 13 percent used candles. Public services included 24 public elementary schools, four night schools, and 10 private primary schools. Only one public high school existed in 1987. There is also the education college (La Cantuta), one health center, and one health post. Chosica has one police station, three post offices, three theaters, a public marketplace, and one stadium.

Overview

In general, Chosica may be considered a middle-size provincial town that is affected, on the one hand, by influences from nearby Lima, which put it in touch with urbanized sociocultural factors and, on the other, by rural influences being brought in as country people migrate from the highlands. This mixture implies relative affluence flowing from the city and poverty from the countryside.

Oaxaca, Mexico: Manuel Esparza

The Setting

The city of Oaxaca lies in the narrow waist of Mexico near the isthmus of Tehuantepec, which borders the Gulf of Mexico on the north and the Pacific Ocean on the south. Two mountain ranges, the eastern and western Mexican Cordilleras which meet in the state of Oaxaca, wind from the high plateaus of central Mexico to the isthmus. From the air, the state appears like a piece of crumpled paper in which, almost by accident, there are some high valleys. At the intersection of one of the largest valleys lies a wide, T-shaped alluvial plain about 700 square kilometers in area. At the intersection of the three arms lies the city of Oaxaca, 1,500 meters above sea level.

The Pre-Hispanic and Colonial Past

The Valley of Oaxaca is one of the few core regions in Mesoamerica from which cultural innovations spread over wide geographic regions. The valley has been inhabited for more than 12,000 years. At its hub is the mountaintop city of Monte Alban (500 B.C. to about A.D. 1500), just a short distance from modern Oaxaca (Blanton 1979). Two thousand years ago Monte Alban and a few other nucleated centers in the valley constituted the main political entity in Mexico's southern highlands (Change 1978).

Zapotec culture evolved from at least 1500 B.C. until the Spanish invasion in the sixteenth century. The Zapotecs developed hieroglyphic writing, a calendrical system, and a distinctive art style that distinguishes their culture from the dozen or more other ethnic groups in the state.

By the time of their arrival in the region in 1521, the Spaniards encountered—in addition to the valley Zapotecs—the Mixtecs who had been in the valley for at least a century, and the omnipresent Aztecs who most likely arrived in 1486 when they established a garrison called Huaxyacac on the site where the Spaniards later founded the city of Antequera, now called Oaxaca, an obvious corruption of the Aztec name (Change 1978:17–18).

At the same time that the Spanish architects laid out the grid-pattern plan of Antequera, Hernán Cortés, the conqueror of Tenochtitlán (Mexico City), was made the marquis of the Valley of Oaxaca, a title that gave him jurisdiction over his domain—most of the valley (Change 1976). Soon, though, Cortés was to lose most of his holdings to the greed and rivalry of his countrymen.

Cortés's holdings were reduced to four *villas* and their subjects. One of those *villas,* an Indian pueblo, was called Villa de Oaxaca and stood next to Antequera, the Spanish city. This fact was decisive for the conflict-riven growth of Antequera. Cortés had jurisdiction over the Aztec and Tlaxcaltecon sections of the settlement in the northern part of Antequera, occupying a semicircle that spread from east to west where the Mixtecs had their territory in the city's southwestern part. The Spanish city would only grow southward. The *Marquesado* was to last through 300 years of colonial domination.

Early Population Trends

The city's layout reflects the Spanish conception of a temporal and spiritual society. A central plaza was bordered by civil and religious buildings on the south and north sides. On the west and east sides of the quadrangle stood business establishments. Covered galleries on all four sides faced the central plaza and fountain.

Despite Spanish efforts to keep the racially different groups segregated from the urban population, from the beginning almost one-third of Antequera's population consisted of Indians who gave a distinctive composition to the city's social web (Esparza 1983). These Indians were mainly Nahuatl speakers from central Mexico and were by far the most highly skilled artisans of the population. The rest of the Indians were Zapotec and Mixtec.

The city of Antequera grew from no more than 2,000 Spaniards at the end of the sixteenth century to fewer than 5,000 Spanish inhabitants in the seventeenth century. On the other hand, the Indian and African communities on the north, west, and east fringes were becoming increasingly crowded. Nonartisan Indians were treated separately, some of them allowed to live only in the south of Antequera.

By the seventeenth century, the Nahuatl hegemony on skills had given way to a growing group of Zapotec and Mixtec Indians. Indian migration to the city continued in the second half of the eighteenth century. In 1792, Indians made up almost 30 percent, or more than 5,000, of the total population of 18,000. The cochineal boom, the textile industry, and the recovery of the Indian population were the main reasons for the mid-eighteenth century's increase. A century later, the city had 185 blocks, 15 of them running north and south, and 18 running east and west. By that time there were 20,000 inhabitants (Berry 1981). All through the nineteenth century the clothing and textile industries occupied more than 26 percent of the labor force, followed by an increasing but related revival in commerce (Esparza 1983). Actually, these two activities characterized the distribution of occupations in the city and have changed little since the late seventeenth century, the main difference being that the labor force occupied in those activities was non-Indian, and in the nineteenth and twentieth centuries the majority were mestizos. By the mid-nineteenth century the city was known as the City of Oaxaca, and the colonial setting and its boundaries changed little until the mid-twentieth century.

The Present Situation

During four centuries of colonial domination Oaxaca was one of the few prominent cities of Mexico. By the second decade of the twentieth century, after a decade of bloodletting revolution, Oaxaca fell from the list of the nation's top 20 cities in population. It is now a secondary city and not ranked among the 20 largest urban settlements (Murphy and Stepick 1991).

For the past four decades Oaxaca has experienced an unprecedented population increase. Gone are the 185 blocks of the mid-nineteenth century as the core of the urban settlement. The urban area on today's maps has jumped the old Indian communities and has moved across *arroyos* and climbed the hills and mountains surrounding the old settlement.

Between 1940 and 1985 Oaxaca averaged more than 4 percent annual growth, compared to 7 to 10 percent in other Mexican cities (Murphy and Stepick 1991). Migration is the main cause of the population increase. Seventy percent of the total migrants come directly from rural communities of the state. Fewer than 10 percent of the city's residents come from outside the state. In the 1970s the increase mainly resulted from people moving from urban areas outside the state as federal agencies expanded, bringing bureaucrats and skilled personnel along with their households. In-migration reached its highest point in the 1950s when the city grew by nearly 60 percent for the decade, close to 5 percent per year. The rate of growth declined to 50 percent for the 1960s, and the same situation prevailed in the 1970s. In the 1980s the growth rate has been approximately 6 percent per year.

Only one-third of household heads are native to the city, but among the economically active population, that figure rises to 45 percent; among the entire population of the city, it reaches 60 percent. One-third of households have owned land for more than 10 years, and 85 percent of household heads have been in the city for ten or more years. Of the adults, 85 percent are married. Almost three-quarters of Oaxaca's households have between three and seven members, the national average being five. Fifty percent of the population is under 17 years old (Murphy and Stepick 1991).

Economic Profile

As in the past, the city of Oaxaca remains primarily a marketing, service, and administrative center for the surrounding rural area. The three main productive activities in the state of Oaxaca are agriculture, crafts, and commerce; the first two are primarily rural-based, while commerce is based in the city of Oaxaca. Within eight blocks surrounding the main plaza are an average of nine commercial establishments per block, and in the next 47 blocks the figure drops to six (Nolasco 1981). Eleven percent of the central city's population are either professionals or owners of commercial establishments, and another 46 percent of household heads are employed in these establishments.

Commerce increased in importance in the 1940s (from 14.3 to 18.3 percent of the work force), did not change by more than 1 percent in the 1950s, and has remained remarkably constant since that decade. The government sector increased notably between 1970 and 1977, from 9.7 to 21.9 percent of the work force. As expected, because of population growth and the city's expansion, the percentage of workers in the construction industry increased from 6.4 to 13.1 between 1970 and 1977, and construction continues to be a major employer (Murphy and Stepick 1991). Industry is virtually absent in the city; only 11.4 percent of the city's workers are in industry, mainly in a plywood factory, small food-processing plants, textile factories, and other, minuscule enterprises. Aside from its geographic isolation from inputs and larger markets, the city of Oaxaca has several major obstacles to industrial development, mainly the lack of water and sufficient electric energy.

Ten percent of workers in the informal sector earn more than the official minimum wage, compared to one-third of workers in the formal sector. Those who earn more than five times the minimum wage are found solely in the formal sector. Nevertheless, more than two-thirds of Oaxaca's formal sector workers earn less than the minimum wage. More significantly, in 1987 more than 60 percent of households had no formal sector workers (Murphy and Stepick 1991). Out of ten Mexican secondary cities surveyed in 1977, Oaxaca had the lowest income levels (Selby, Murphy, and Lorenzen in press). Thirty percent of those categorized as the Very Poor in a four-class division by Murphy and Stepick (1991) earned less than the minimum wage; as a group, they received just over 10 percent of the city's total income. The remaining 70 percent earned more than the official minimum salary.

Minimum wage is a misleading measure of economic sufficiency, however, since it is generally acknowledged to be only a relative scale of value. A family cannot live on one minimum wage in Mexico. Perhaps a more realistic measurement was established in 1977 by FOVI, a bank-sponsored and government-regulated fund that provided housing loans to low-income workers. FOVI calculated that a household must earn 1.8 times the local minimum salary to guarantee a subsidized loan (Murphy and Stepick 1991). By this standard, 65 percent of Oaxaca's population does not earn enough income. The highest income group, completely self-sufficient by FOVI standards, constitutes only 7 percent of the city's population and earns 25 percent of the city's income.

Housing

The rate of population growth in the city of Oaxaca in the 1980s has been approximately 5 percent per year, and it will continue to grow for some time if we consider that most households are still in the childbearing stage and that one-half of the city's population is under 17 years of age. These facts and the city's economic situation explain how people obtain housing. Two characteristics define the pattern of housing in Oaxaca. First, the real estate market is almost completely absent. Second, squatter settlements constitute more than half of the city's area (Murphy and Stepick 1991). Much of the land surrounding the city itself is communal, and some is *ejido* land that cannot legally be sold (Simpson 1937). By the mid-1970s, more than 60 percent of the urban area of Oaxaca was covered with housing that was on land with unclear legal title (Murphy 1985). Cheap prices and easy terms attract people to buy land without services such as water and electricity.

Households construct housing by buying building materials little by little and by constructing their own homes. More specialized operations like plumbing and wiring are contracted out. The process of building a three-room house with an attached kitchen begins when the household moves into a single room. The whole process might take 15 years, provided that the household head continues to hold a steady job (Murphy and Stepick 1991).

Government-sponsored housing covers only 16.8 percent of the population's needs (Murphy and Stepick 1991). These projects try to meet the needs of workers in the formal sector by subsidizing housing for those who have enough income to meet mortgage payments. Programs for formal sector workers also cover workers in the public sector. In general, households legally have to live in these houses once they have acquired them through a payroll deduction plan, but it is not uncommon for people to keep living in their former houses outside of the city center while they rent out the new houses, thus obtaining extra income and providing housing to friends and relatives. This is another example of the irregular market in which holders rent and even sell their properties, just as villagers in rural areas sell communal lands.

The middle and upper classes have their own neighborhoods, and, as expected, they can afford to build their houses through a contractor and often with the services of an architect, who in turn has a contractor who supervises the *maestros* and *peons*. These better-off household heads are employed in the economy's white-collar sector (64 percent) and represent only 8.2 percent of the city's population (Murphy and Stepick 1991).

Summary

The provincial city of Oaxaca is the state capital of a relatively poor region of Mexico. Economically, it falls below the average for the country as a whole. With respect to housing and those factors associated with the accumulation of domestic assets, Oaxaca has been characterized in recent years by a high percentage of self-constructed housing that began as informal houses built in squatter settlements on the old city's fringes. Incomes are relatively low, and the informal economy furnishes the economic base for a large part of the population. Thus, Oaxaca falls below Mexico's national average on the median value of domestic assets held by households.

Santa Barbara, United States: Dennis S. Mileti

The Setting

The city of Santa Barbara lies at the northernmost point of the area known as southern California. It is located on the coast, and it borders on the Pacific Ocean. The city is about a 1.5-hour drive north of Los Angeles and is in the Goleta Valley. The Santa Ynez Mountains are at its eastern edge. Montecito, Summerland, and Carpinteria are neighboring cities that share the valley.

History

Santa Barbara began with the Chumash Indians, who settled in the area about 10,000 years ago. These Indians are known for an extremely distinctive language, sandstone pictographs, an advanced system of trade and commerce, and innovative forms of architecture.

João Rodrigues Cabrillo, a Portuguese navigator, was the first European to set foot on the California coast. He claimed it for Spain in 1542. When Sebastian Vizcaino's ship anchored offshore in 1602 on the feast day of St. Barbara, the ship's priest named the channel and land area in honor of the patron saint of mariners. The area has been known as Santa Barbara since December 4, 1602.

In April 1782 the Santa Barbara *Presidio Real* (Royal Fortress) was formally established in ceremonies conducted by Father Junipero Serra. The Santa Barbara Royal Presidio was the fourth and last military outpost built for the Spanish empire in the New World; the others were in San Diego, San Francisco, and Monterey. Santa Barbara's Presidio was the first permanent settlement for Europeans in the area. José Francisco Ortega was appointed *commandante* for the area by the Spanish empire. He ruled from Santa Barbara and acted as military and civilian administrator, treasurer, and postmaster for the entire district, which extended from Santa Ynez north of San Francisco to the pueblo of Los Angeles in the south.

During the first 70 years of Santa Barbara's modern existence, the flags of Spain, Mexico, independent California, and the United States flew at the Presidio. Earthquakes in 1806 and 1812 caused considerable damage, and by the 1840s much of the Presidio had fallen into ruin, its chapel being dismantled in 1855.

On December 4, 1786, Father Lasuen of the Franciscan order established Mission Santa Barbara, the tenth of the California missions. The mission church was destroyed by the earthquake in 1812. Its replacement was finished in 1820. Damaged by an earthquake on June 29, 1925, and subsequently repaired, the church remains standing today.

The first American settler in Santa Barbara arrived in 1817. In 1845 the Mexican-American War broke out, and the following year Mexico surrendered Santa Barbara to American forces. The city was retaken by Mexican forces a few months later. Several months thereafter, the city was regained by the Americans and has been a part of the United States since then. Military forces occupied the city from 1847 to 1849 and used the Presidio as a corral. On April 9, 1850, Santa Barbara was incorporated as a city by an act of the new California legislature. It became a real seaport in 1871 when Stearns Wharf was completed. In the late 1850s an opera house was constructed that was southern California's largest adobe structure.

The earthquake of 1925 caused 11 deaths, millions of dollars in property damage, and dramatically altered the completion of Santa Barbara. Immediately after the temblor, the city, urged on by the community arts association, set up an architectural board of review. Thus, present-day Santa Barbara evolved from strict architectural control.

Economic and Population Profile

The largest not-for-profit employer in the area is the University of California at Santa Barbara with a total annual payroll of $86.7 million, 2,879 employees, and a student body of 18,000. The largest for-profit firm is Santa Barbara Research Center with an annual payroll of $63 million and 2,200 employees. High-technology industry dominates the for-profit economic sector; in 1984, 77 percent of the largest employers in the area were high-tech firms.

Some 245 acres within the city limits are zoned for light industry; this acreage includes two industrial parks. However, it was not until the first half of the 1960s that the area's economic structure moved from primarily agricultural to industrial. Agriculture still contributes a large measure to the area's economy; orchids, avocados, citrus fruits, livestock, and field crops are among the principal agricultural products.

The labor force in the Santa Barbara area numbered 39,158 people in 1980; 62.1 percent were 16 years of age and over, and 52.2 percent were female. The labor force was composed of 37,315 employed and 1,843 unemployed; 27,136 (72.7 percent) of those who were employed worked in the private sector. Occupational categories for the employed were distributed as follows: 10,728 (28.7 percent) managerial and professional occupations; 11,617 (31.1 percent) technical, sales, and administrative; 5,426 (14.5 percent) service; 1,356 (3.6 percent) farm; 4,016 (10.8 percent) production; and 3,672 (9.8 percent) laborer. About half (52.6 percent) of families had two or more workers; about one-third (30.1 percent) of families, one worker, and 17.3 percent of families, no workers.

Median 1980 household income was $15,445, and mean household income was $20,376. Household income by category was distributed as follows: 4,164 (12.8 percent) less than $5,000; 2,911 (8.9 percent) $5,000 to $7,499; 3,049 (9.4 percent) $7,500 to $9,999; 5,689 (17.5 percent) $10,000 to $14,999; 4,615 (14.2 percent) $15,000 to $19,999; 3,424 (10.5 percent)

$20,000 to $24,999; 4,184 (12.9 percent) $25,000 to $34,999; 2,626 (8.1 percent) $35,000 to $49,999; and 1,880 (5.8 percent) $50,000 and more. The per capita income of non-institutionalized persons was $9,173. Of the 37,315 employed persons ten years of age and over, 2,471 (6.6 percent) were unemployed for 15 weeks or more.

Of the 56,269 people 25 years old and over, 8,334 (14.8 percent) had an education of eight years or less; 5,861 (10.4 percent), three years of high school or less; 14,811 (26.3 percent), high school graduates; 11,537 (20.5 percent), some college; and 14,560 (25.9 percent), college graduates. Less than half (47.1 percent) of the population of 84,501 were male, while 52.9 percent were female. The age structure of the population was 4,413 (5.2 percent), under five years; 8,750 (10.3 percent), five to 14 years; 52,762 (62.4 percent), 15 to 59 years; 4,039 (4.8 percent), 60 to 64 years; and 14,547 (17.2 percent), 65 years and older. Some 19.5 percent of the population were of Spanish origin, 75.5 percent were white, 23.5 percent were black, and 1 percent were of other racial/ethnic origins.

The economic and demographic characteristics of the city of Santa Barbara are somewhat misleading. The city is contiguous with some of the most affluent economic areas in California. For example, developments to its north are havens for millionaires, and former president Ronald Reagan's ranch is in the hills above the city. But the city itself is largely inhabited by people of less affluence.

Housing Characteristics

There were 33,925 total housing units in the city of Santa Barbara. Of these, 13,532 (39.9 percent) were owner-occupied. Whites resided in 12,284 (90.8 percent) of the owner-occupied units, while blacks occupied 209 (1.5 percent) of these units, and 1,039 (7.7 percent) were occupied by other racial/ethnic groups. Only four housing units in the city lacked complete plumbing, and all of these were renter-occupied. The median number of rooms in year-round housing units was 5.2; however, about 43.6 percent of these units had six or more rooms. Occupancy ratio medians were 2.03 for occupied housing units, 2.13 for owner-occupied units, and 1.87 for renter-occupied units. The median housing unit value in 1980 was $195,500, with 48.2 percent of all units worth above $200,000.

Some 61.4 percent of year-round housing units had one complete bathroom, 36.1 percent one and one-half or more bathrooms, and 2.5 percent no bathroom or only a half-bath. Almost all housing units (97 percent) had complete kitchen facilities, while 3 percent did not. The source of water for housing units was provided almost exclusively by a public system or private company (33,853 units), while 18 units obtained water from individually drilled wells, 13 units from an individually dug well, and 16 units from some other source. Public sewers took care of disposal for 33,329 units, a septic tank or cesspool for 403 units, and other means for 168 units.

Heat was provided in a variety of ways. Steam or hot water heat was used in 1,018 units; 10,947 had a central warm air furnace; 397 units used an electric heat pump; 4,947 units used built-in electric units; 8,066 units were heated by a floor, wall, or pipeless furnace; 6,504 units had room heaters with a flue; 1,089 units had room heaters without a flue; 638 units obtained heat from a fireplace, stove, or portable room heater; and 284 units had no heat source. Telephones were in all but 4.6 percent of the city's housing units.

Of the 33,900 year-round housing units in Santa Barbara, 16,020 were single detached units, 1,345 single attached units, 1,928 two-unit structures, 2,405 three- and four-unit structures, 11,842 had five or more unit structures, and 360 were mobile homes or trailers.

Of these 33,900 housing units, 8,995 were built in 1939 or earlier; 3,853 were built from 1940 to 1949; 7,527 from 1950 to 1959; 8,355 from 1960 to 1969; 3,114 from 1970 to 1974; 1,606 from 1975 to 1978; and 450 from 1979 to March 1980. Most (33.4 percent) housing units had one to three stories, while 430 had four stories or more. Of those with four or more stories, 24 units did not have elevators. There were no bedrooms in 2,455 housing units; 9,661 had one bedroom; 11,708, two bedrooms; 7,565, three bedrooms; 2,044, four bedrooms; and 467, five or more bedrooms. Of the 32,509 occupied housing units, 26,129 were heated by utility gas; 215 used bottled or tank gas; 5,597, electric heat; 85, fuel oil or kerosene; 187, wood; 30, some other fuel source; and 271, no fuel or heat. Water was heated with utility gas in 27,316 units; bottled or tank gas was used in 526 units, electricity in 4,451 units, fuel oil or kerosene in 34 units, other fuel types in 41 units, and in 111 units no fuel was used to heat water.

Overview

Santa Barbara has the reputation of being an extremely affluent city located in an affluent state. A better description of the city itself is that it is of slightly higher income than average, surrounded by a rich periphery. Its institutions reflect this state of affairs, but the households within the city itself are not remarkably different from those in most California small cities as evidenced by the median household incomes of Santa Barbara's residents. It departs from the average city mainly because of the nature of its economic base, which rests on high-tech industry and on services offered to the affluent population living around its fringes.

Slavonski Brod, Yugoslavia: Josip Obradovic

History

Slavonski Brod is situated in Croatia in the eastern part of the valley that extends from Zagreb toward Belgrade. At the intersection of several main roads to Belgrade, as well as north to Hungary and south to other parts of Yugoslavia, Slavonski Brod has always been an important border town linking Croatia and Bosnia.

On its present site, the old Roman city of Morsonia was founded, and the passing stream is still called after this first city name: Mrsunja. Archaeological excavations have dated Morsonia as far back as the time of Constantine.

During the eleventh and twelfth centuries Morsonia was replaced by a fort, Vukovac, which held a significant commercial and strategic position on the River Sava. Vukovac was later torn down during Turkish invasions, but because of its highly favorable defensive and strategic position, Fort Vukovac was frequently restored and rebuilt, first by Croatian and later by Austro-Hungarian kings. The fort itself was inhabited by soldiers only, but since it provided security for the neighboring districts, it became a center toward which peasants, merchants, and craftsmen migrated and settled on surrounding lands.

In 1550 the Turks succeeded in capturing the fort and the small town by the name of Brod Na Savi (the vessel on River Sava) that flourished by its side. Turks reigned in these parts up to 1691. During their rule, the fort was rebuilt and further fortified, but the surrounding population diminished. When the Turks finally left the region at the end of the seventeenth century, Brod Na Savi was inhabited by a population of only 1,500.

For the better part of the eighteenth century the town was under the military command of the Austro-Hungarian monarchy. It still fulfilled a militarily defensive function, a role to which its inhabitants were strongly opposed. They continually tried to achieve the status of a free city, governed by a civilian government. This was finally achieved in 1753, but only for a short time. In 1787 the town was again under military rule, as defense against the Turks once more became a necessity. Wars against the Turks and Napoleon caused great damage to the city, and its population was decimated, its economy and crafts ruined, and its roads rendered unusable. Military rule was finally discontinued in 1820 when Brod Na Savi was for a second time made a free city by the court.

A gradual rise from the ashes then took place. Various craftsmen and merchants opened businesses, and the economy began to develop little by little. By the beginning of the twentieth century, Slavonski Brod was encroaching on both sides of the River Sava and boasted a population of 4,500. This prosperity was, however, short-lived. World War I made the town into a military fortress again. At the end of the war the Austro-Hungarian empire was divided into several parts. One part was combined with the kingdom of Serbia to form a new country, at first called the country of Serbs, Croats, and Slovenes, and afterward the kingdom of Yugoslavia. Brod Na Savi became a part of Yugoslavia, and between the two world wars it was finally reached by the Industrial Revolution. The industries of metal manufacturing and wood processing began to flourish. Soon, however, the city was again involved in military conflict.

World War II had an especially heavy impact on Brod Na Savi. In fact, the city was almost completely demolished and had to start from the ashes again. After World War II, the new republic of Yugoslavia was constituted with the Communist party in control of the government. Industry, commerce, and agriculture were nationalized. The new country's main aim was industrialization by all means possible. By a system of political pressures, villagers were motivated to leave their villages to join the industrial work force. As a consequence, a rapid growth of cities took place. As part of the reorganization of Yugoslavia, Brod Na Savi was divided administratively into two towns: Slavonski Brod on the north bank of the River Sava was part of the republic of Croatia, and Bosanski Brod on the south side was a part of the republic of Bosnia and Herzegovina. The larger part of the former town Brod Na Savi was contained in Slavonski Brod. Under the new regime it began to develop as a large industrial center. Heavy investments were put into the metal- and wood-processing industries. In addition, the city became a significant agroindustrial center with the development of food-processing plants.

Current Economy

Modern Slavonski Brod is primarily an industrial town. According to the 1981 census, 47,270 people lived there. In the neighboring villages the number of inhabitants was 53,366, meaning that the agricultural population immediately surrounding the city was quite large. Of the city's population, 18,934 are employed within the city; the other 20,924 employees who work in the city come from surrounding villages and travel daily to Slavonski Brod to work.

It is difficult to estimate the present value of per capita production in Slavonski Brod because of the enormous inflation that has taken place in Yugoslavia since 1985. Some estimates put it between $2,700 and $3,000 (U.S.), which is lower than the level of per capita productivity for Croatia, but on a level with Yugoslavia as a whole.

Industry was the main source of income, and in 1988 some 49.8 percent of local income came from industry. Agriculture was in second place (15.2 percent) and transportation third (13.4 percent). The remaining parts of local income were contributed by civil engineering, commerce, the restaurant industry, and crafts. It is important to mention that only 8.92 percent of local income came from the private sector, while everything else came from the socialized economy. The major part of Slavonski Brod's economic output stemmed from metal manufacturing of machine tools, tractors, and combines, and production of railway engines and cars.

Slavonski Brod can be described as a typical Yugoslav industrial town that was swiftly transformed from a provincial town to a significant industrial center. In spite of this development, the population in the town, and especially in its vicinity, is rural in cultural orientation.

Demographic and Social Aspects

To form a better picture of Slavonski Brod, it is important to examine its demographic and social characteristics in addition to its economy. According to 1988 data, the birthrate was 15.9 per 1,000 inhabitants. This was somewhat higher than the average for Croatia (12.9 per 1,000 inhabitants) and can be explained by the rural character and traditional culture of the town's inhabitants. Population growth produced by births alone was 5.6 per 1,000 inhabitants in 1988, while in all Croatia it was only 1.8 per 1,000. The population in Croatia is stagnant except in areas that preserve traditional cultural patterns such as Slavonski Brod.

In 1988 there were eight stillbirths per 1,000 births in Slavonski Brod compared to 5.1 stillbirths per 1,000 births in Croatia. Other demographic data point to a below-average health status. For instance, the city had a higher number of deaths of infants younger than six days, and of deaths of infants younger than one year, than in the rest of Croatia—21 deaths per 1,000 children born in Slavonski Brod and 15.8 per 1,000 in Croatia. All of these are important indicators of lower-than-average prenatal and postnatal care and point not only to a lower level of health standards, but to a lower level of health education. It also could indicate a lower quality of preparation of food and sanitation than in the rest of Croatia.

Educational Aspects

According to the census in 1981, 5 percent of the population aged ten and older was illiterate. This was less than the average for Croatia (6 percent) or all of Yugoslavia (11 percent). This low percentage for Slavonski Brod probably resulted from its urban population, while the average for Croatia included the rural population. The illiteracy rate in the whole of Yugoslavia was higher because of the inclusion of the country's southern parts, which are economically and socially less developed.

In Slavonski Brod, as well as in Croatia and Yugoslavia, the percentage of illiterate women was higher than men in 1981 (8 percent women and 7 percent men). The breakdown by age showed that most illiterate people (more than 60 percent) were older than 55 years. This relatively high level of literacy is one of the most significant achievements of postwar social and economic development. To fully assess the magnitude of this success, it should be noted that immediately after World War II the illiteracy rate in the whole of Yugoslavia (Slavonski Brod included) was 80 percent! Today, illiteracy has been practically eliminated in Croatia, but it is still high in some lesser-developed regions of Yugoslavia.

Following World War II, impressive changes took place in the general population's level of education. In 1988 the number of pupils in secondary schools in Slavonski Brod was 5,045, representing 98 percent of all pupils who finished elementary school (eight years). In the 1990s the population of Slavonski Brod will have 12 years of schooling on average. In addition to secondary schools, Slavonski Brod has a Workers' and People's University with an engineering faculty and 600 students as well as adult and continuing education courses.

Slavonski Brod also has a theater, a museum, a library, several cinemas, and a large medical center. Because of extensive state financial support, there are varied regular cultural activities in the town, including art exhibitions, theatrical groups on tour, and concerts. The town also has its own radio station, newspapers, and a book publishing company. Several sports clubs and societies are active.

Summary

Slavonski Brod is a typical Yugoslav small city that was transformed after World War II into a significant industrial center. Still, the rural and traditional character of its population is strong. Many inhabitants might be considered half-rural and half-urban, so the prevailing mentality is one of a provincial town.

Söke, Turkey: Aydin Germen

The River Meander, in a westward course toward the Aegean Sea, passes between the site of ancient Miletus and present Söke.[1] During historical times, silt from the river filled a gulf some 20 miles wide and 30 miles long. The geological term for such gulfs is *ria*,[2] describing something akin to but different from fjords. Such a coastline naturally provides many good port locations. The rivers, on the other hand, have clogged the ports and have formed fertile valleys.

Söke itself may have been at the apex of the Latmian Gulf following the last Ice Age. The advance of alluvium forming the broad plain near the city has been documented for several historical periods. Until recent decades, boats were used on the plain's small lakes, and water was pumped from one lake to another for irrigation. The delta's present edge still advances 40 feet per year. I walked in the sea for a couple of miles on the frighteningly soft bottom some fifteen years ago. Some of the fishnets located in the sea at that time have been replaced by land.

Söke is in a region once occupied by many important ancient cities. While the destruction and abandonment of many of these cities is attributable to other causes, there also has been some earthquake damage. One example is the Temple of Apollo at Didyma, several miles out of Miletus, which was built over more than two centuries by a league of cities, but never completed because of its expense. It thus may have missed being included among the ancient world's Seven Wonders (it was made a ruin much later by a known earthquake). One ancient wonder, however, was located in another of Söke's neighboring cities: the Temple of Artemis (Diana) in Ephesus. This is Artemis country, and there was another Artemisium in another immediately neighboring city, Magnesia on the Meander. According to archaeologists and art historians, this temple is as important as the Temple of Apollo. Two other ancient Wonders are located within 40 and 100 miles of Söke.[3]

An immediate neighbor is modern Kusadasi, a vast, linear tourist city on the seashore. Before the proliferation of hotels, the initial attraction of this port town was the House of Mary, Mother of Christ, recently and officially so defined by the Roman Catholic Church. The house is actually on a mountaintop near the ancient city of Ephesus.

The natural attractions and the processes of land formation mentioned above have been major influences on the region's settlement, urbanization, and economic base. The river here brings water, and, along with it, the soil from several provinces. Those tributaries supplying the river's headwaters are under snow cover in winter, but melting snow does not outlast the rainless summer. Still, these plains suffer no water shortage. The county gets abundant rainfall of 40 inches per year, and the dry summer perfectly suits the boll and the harvesting of cotton, the leading crop. The varied lay of the land suits both water-consuming cotton on the bottom terrain and tobacco, a second major crop, on the well-drained foothills. Cotton must have arrived here very early and is at least datable to the Selçuk Turkish period. Around Söke, industry-oriented crops take precedence over others. Tobacco cultivation is a small familial operation.[4]

Licorice (a mainstay of American confectionery), medicaments, and beverages since the mid-nineteenth century and well into more recent times must all have come from this area. Cotton and licorice are seen to have had a leading role in the railroad's arrival in this district in 1889. The primacy of the railway, however, has long been superseded by the highway. Today Söke is 1.5 hours by car from an international airport.

While the nearby metropolis, Izmir, may increase to a population of 3 million in coming years, Söke's neighboring cities range in size from more than 20,000 to less than 200,000 and are roughly 15 to 50 miles away. All are very distant psychologically from the large city, and all function rather well. Until recently, Söke was known as a city with absentee cotton landlords, a low-income proletariat, and a population of uncohesive in-migrants.

The 1985 sample survey for this study, together with a cursory study of history and further visits since 1985, partially confirm this image, and partially fail to do so. Today as one enters the town, the medians in wider stretches of the roads are centered with geraniums and other plants in bloom throughout the year. Olive groves and single olive trees continue into the city. Nut Pine (*Pinus pinea*) on the lower elevations and cypresses in the outlying districts create a resemblance to Italian or Greek landscapes. One short avenue is lined with exotic and imposing palm trees.

Its architecture shows that the town is of recent growth. Apartment buildings (an average of six stories) have a style which approximates that of the leading cities of the country more than other county seats. This, of course, does not make them any lovelier. A few housing projects are higher than six stories. There seem to be, proportionately, as many low buildings in the town center as in many peripheral residential areas. In this center is found a profusion of small, narrow shops, along Turkish traditional lines. This central business area is more extensive and livelier than in most towns of comparable size in the rest of the country.

Population

There were close to 45,000 people in Söke at the time of our sample survey, 1985, with a slight majority of males. This total was up from 9,300 in 1927, 13,400 in 1950, and 23,600 in 1960. The rate of increase in the urban area was only slightly higher than in the surrounding villages on the river plain. This population growth is usually assigned to an increase in cotton culture and activities related to it, even though many workers in the cotton fields are seasonally employed. In-migration from outside the province, some of which is not associated with cotton, includes people whose land was expropriated for the purposes of the gigantic Euphrates River project in eastern Turkey. These migrants arrived after the 1985 census and the survey for this study. There were earlier migrations from Peloponnesus in Greece (1829), from Crete (1899), and from Bulgaria over the past five decades, all contributing a minor part in Söke's growth.

For two reasons, squatting, which is a pattern found in many rapidly growing cities, is not important in Söke. First, the survey gave the impression that for a town which has grown rapidly and has rather large industry, squatting is minimal. Second, it is my opinion that in Turkey the boundary between squatting and nonsquatting is becoming ever more indistinct. In Turkey by 1971, nine types of squatting could be counted on the basis of legal and other criteria. It may be agreed that squatting is defined legally, when, among other things, we distinguish between property law and town planning law, but as the professional or other qualities of town planning become questionable, the lines separating squatting from other types of settlement become questionable as well.

The Economy

I will not discuss the "informal sector," first, because I have not come across noticeable signs of it, and second, because I find such analysis fraught with improper terminology and concepts.

The following conversation in May 1990 provides one picture of Söke:

AG: More than three decades ago we used to be told there were three, or say five, "real rich" families in Söke; in the sample three seemed rich to us, and thus there must be nine to ten such families?

HO: There must be a thousand at least.

AG: Do you mean families or persons?

HO: Now this is very hard to say because practically they all descend from a single man, or say two, in the nineteenth century, and there are many marriage complications.

Later in the conversation we decided we could perhaps not go below the figure of 500 relatively well-to-do people; better to think of them as persons rather than families. The number has greatly swollen in recent years to that level because of people who have sold large tracts of land to tourism establishments in the vicinity and people who operate such firms, there being few other sources of wealth.

HO: "There is no middle class in Söke." Some findings in the assets survey support this view, but some do not. HO: "Söke is always very late in acquiring amenities or new facilities." This is not true by any means when I think of the more than 100 county seats I visited during the summer of 1989 in eastern Turkey and its neighboring areas.

Over the past four decades, old money from cotton has been going into industry. In the 1950s the central government started the cement industry as a boon to economic development. In operation for less than three decades, it is now a large establishment with an annual capacity of 220,000 tons. With the final transfer of government shares, it is now a totally private enterprise. A yarn and textile factory is by far the largest employer in Söke. The yarn business is export-oriented, and the product is appreciated in Europe. A flour factory is the third-largest employer. In addition, a large prefab housing establishment standing alone on the river plain several miles to the south of Söke employs more than 1,100 people.

There are numerous ginning mills and olive oil presses in Söke. A small industrial cooperative also has created two sites, totaling 117 acres, where many small businesses are located. In keeping with national tradition, the town organizes street markets twice a week, with differing clientele depending on time and location. The clientele includes seasonal workers, construction workers, tourists, summer home residents, and government employees.

The base for Söke's industry is agricultural land. Fruits and olives, while they have minor importance in the town's economy, take up more than one-fourth of the county's total land area, and the important field crops take one-third.

Another one-third is forest land. The townspeople associate the development of the cotton industry with the 1950s, but the arrival of the railway in the nineteenth century, several Turkish *konaks* (mansions) and several townhouses with the elegant lines of late nineteenth-century Greek architecture, and two substantial mosques, one from the beginning and the other from the end of the eighteenth century, attest to the earlier development of a strong economic base. These data stand in contrast with the earliest available census figures on population.

The town's educational system appears remarkable in three respects. First, more than half of the secondary schools are addressed to the industrial and agricultural activities mentioned above, and there is active or prospective co-operation between the producers and the schools, not to mention increased job opportunities. In contrast, for the nation in general it has been difficult until now to concentrate on vocational education. Second, the very number of these lyceums (formally equivalent to junior colleges in the United States), including both the technical and the classical, is noticeable. There are eight lyceums (or, including those provisionally administered together with others, ten lyceums) in a town of this size. Third, few of these schools were started without a substantial contribution by well-to-do families. This is far from being the rule in other Turkish towns. At an appropriate time these schools are taken into the public system. The vocational system includes industrial techniques, tourism, commerce, and girls' vocational training. The agricultural school has expanded into biogas (computerized measurement techniques) and has established test laboratories.

Udine, Italy: Carlo Pelanda

The city of Udine is in the extreme northeast of Italy, very close to the borders of both Yugoslavia and Austria. The urban settlement lies on a small hill in the center of the Friuli Plain, bordered on the north and east by the Prealps and Alps. The plain extends far to the west, but is limited on the south by the Adriatic Sea. The town's strategic location in the geographical center of the populated plain, at the crossing of several historic routes of communication that lead from the Adriatic Sea to the Padana Plain and to central Europe through narrow alpine valleys, is closely related to its historical and sociopolitical evolution.

Historical Notes

The town's exact origin is not known, and the earliest document explicitly confirming its existence dates to A.D. 983. An imperial diploma confirms the affiliation of the small village and its castle with the powerful patriarch of Aquileia, the ruler of an important Roman city on the northern Adriatic coast. Under the succeeding patriarchs' rule, the city was accorded the status of *libero comune,* allowing considerable political autonomy and many economic privileges. Thanks to its favorable geographical position, Udine experienced rapid economic and urban development between the twelfth and fifteenth centuries. In the confrontation between the Austrian empire and the republic of Venice for control of the area, the town's rapid growth led to a period of violent struggle among rich families for political domination. A long period of internecine conflict and riots characterized Udine's life throughout the fourteenth and fifteenth centuries, during which the town was dominated by different foreign powers until its eventual annexation by the republic of Venice in 1420. In spite of receiving the status of the area's capital under Venetian domination, the city suffered a lengthy period of economic decay. It was only in the eighteenth century that the city's fortunes turned again for the better, and Udine became an important economic, cultural, and artistic center.

After the fall of the Venetian republic in 1797, Udine passed under the control of the Austrian empire and, for a short period during the Napoleonic Wars, was occupied by French troops. The town took part in the insurrection of 1848, and a provisional pro-Italian government ruled for a few weeks before the town was bombarded and reconquered by the Austrians. The anti-Austrian movement remained highly active even after the town's reunion with the kingdom of Italy. This reunion also triggered a new period of economic and industrial development. During World War I, after the Italian retreat in 1917, the town was occupied and severely damaged by the Germans. In 1918, before the arrival of the Italian army and after a year of passive resistance, a popular insurrection succeeded in liberating the city. Between the two world wars, the government promoted Udine's role as an important communication node, and private commercial and industrial activities grew in number and importance. Occupied again by the Germans in World War II, the town reasserted its traditional anti-German feeling and played an important role in the anti-Nazi resistance. In 1945, it again succeeded in liberating itself from occupation, preventing the retreating Germans from destroying economic and civilian facilities.

Present Situation

Today Udine is a medium-size Italian city, with a population of about 100,000 inhabitants (98,872; 53.1 percent females, 46.9 percent males). After a century of continuous population growth, Udine has entered a phase of stability and of gradual deindustrialization in favor of the industrialization of the province's surrounding rural areas. The increase in the population's average age is a further sign of demographic decline. At present, about 25.1 percent of the residents are older than 60, the standard age for retirement in Italy. This aging pattern is consistent with a general Italian trend. The number of births per 1,000 population per year is 7.4, while the corresponding death rate is 11.7.

Udine is the administrative capital (county seat) of a broad province. It is served by a medium-size airport with national and some international connections and is joined to the rest of the country and to Austria by a recently completed four-lane highway. It is also located on several railway lines, the first built in the nineteenth century. These railway lines were highly important in the town's economic development. The city is also connected with its province by a busy public bus service.

Udine functions as the bureaucratic, commercial, cultural, and financial center for the entire region. This dominance is evident in structural economic terms since the city shows an increasing specialization in the service sector. Of 40,018 employed residents (male, 62 percent; female, 38 percent), 540 are occupied in agricultural activities (1.3 percent), 8,356 in industrial activities (20.9 percent), and 31,122 in services (77.8 percent). The unemployment rate in the mid-eighties was about 2.5 percent. Average income ranked sixteenth among the 95 Italian county seats, and the region's net income was seventh among 21 regions. There has been, however, evidence of a slowdown of Udine's development pace after 1980.

Urban Development and Characteristics

The present territorial configuration of the Udine area and of Friuli derives from a long history of human intervention. Before the Roman conquest, the entire area was covered by an especially thick forest, to the point that the region's Latin name was *Silva Lupanica* (wolves' forest). The complex work of deforestation and *bonifica* promoted by the Romans was almost completely lost after the empire's decline and fall, and new activity would not be undertaken until the turn of the millennium.

Udine itself grew out of preexisting small, inhabited hamlets. The town's urban settlement began with construction of a canal system to provide the small village with necessary water. Its rapid economic development, and the political events occurring in the thirteenth century, led to construction on a low hilltop of a small fortress, which was demolished in the fourteenth century to make room for the present larger castle and encircling walls. One century later, a new, larger wall was built, both to satisfy the needs of the increased number of inhabitants and for fiscal reasons. Indeed, the town walls were conceived of more as customs barriers than as defensive devices.

The two circles of walls distinguish three distinct types of urban environments. The historical center coincides with the area of the town originally included within the first two circles of walls, both of which were demolished in the nineteenth century to make room for a loop of boulevards. The historical center is characterized by several architectonic strata in a configuration typical of Italian cities with medieval origins. Ancient and historical buildings stand side by side with modern structures. The mixture of styles is also a consequence of numerous disruptive events over the centuries. These included natural disasters, earthquakes and floods, and the consequences of invasions and bombardments during World War I. Most official buildings are located in the central area, together with the traditional commercial downtown. A recent reconstruction of ancient buildings has transformed the historic center into a high-income residential and business district, expelling the original lower-class inhabitants toward the periphery.

The semicentral area corresponds to the part of the territory included within the city limits when the most recent surrounding walls were completed at the beginning of the sixteenth century. Originally composed of a host of small, modest farm units, the area maintained its rural characteristics until the end of the 1800s. Most buildings were simple, low, one- or two-story farmhouses, usually built at the edge of the road, with relatively large farming areas behind them. Part of this area within the walls was occupied by vegetable gardens, monasteries, cemeteries, and the famous ancient public park, referred to by Boccaccio in the *Decameron*. As a consequence of a fast-growing population and the urbanization of many residents from the surrounding countryside, this area was subject to a rapid, unplanned chaotic urbanization process at the end of the nineteenth century.

Nowadays, most buildings in this area of Udine are private, upper-middle-class homes, with a mixture of detached houses and century-old apartment complexes. The city's impressive development in the twentieth century expanded its limits far beyond the perimeter of the surrounding walls that were sufficient to contain it for almost 500 years. New housing developments have risen in the now semiperipheral zone, which at present constitutes a mix of middle-class and low-income residential neighborhoods. Beyond this semi-peripheral area lies the industrial periphery that, in its expansion since the late 1950s, has come to encompass within the urban area several villages that once surrounded the older city.

Udine's general housing situation is related to both the city's historical char-acteristics and to certain sociopolitical contingencies. The average number of occupants per room in housing units in the residential nuclei is 0.59. Conser-vative official figures indicate that of a total of 39,775 housing units, at least 10 percent are not occupied because of the effects of rent control on the income received by landlords who prefer not to rent at current prices. The demographic composition and fragmentation of families are other reasons for the current housing situation.

The general quality of housing in Udine reflects the city's relatively high economic status. Almost all houses have running water and electrical power, and more than 70 percent of the families have private telephones. Ninety-seven percent of the houses have a private bath, and 80 percent have central or in-dependent heating, while 20 percent have stoves. A great deal of restoration, especially of ancient buildings in the historical center, has transformed old and unhealthy housing into luxury residences with modern comforts.

These descriptions demonstrate that there is considerable variability among the sample cities in their economic, social, and cultural characteristics and in their representativeness of the countries in which they are located. At the same time, they meet the criteria required for a testing of the Domestic Assets Scale. Obvi-ously, the sample does not include cities from Africa or Asia and other areas of the world where unanticipated domestic assets items may yet be encountered. For this reason, no claims can yet be made that this instrument will be useful outside the general cultural areas where it was tested in this study.

Endnotes

1. The first syllable in Söke, with the umlaut, is pronounced as in German, or as "eu" in French, or as in English "urge," but in English does not seem producible without the "r." This sound exists only in a few other languages, including Mongo-lian, Scandinavian, and Chinese. The final "e" is as in "pet." The name apparently derives from someone in the early fourteenth century. The river's name is the basis of the English verb "to meander" and its derived usages: in Greek, Maiandros; in Turkish, Menderes. The words "magnetism" and "magnesium" and their deriva-

tives are not assigned to either of the Magnesias in Asia Minor, but to the city in Thessaly.

2. *Ria* derives from Spanish (inlet), better thought of as an estuary, and is to be distinguished from fjords by its conical form with an apex to the land side, its broadening and deepening toward the sea, and its comparatively shorter length. The sinking of the Aegean Sea has been associated with the legendary Lost Continent of Atlantis.

3. Accounts of the classical times, and of the geological framework, and dates of earthquakes can be found only in scattered literature. Statistics are available nationally or through the chamber of commerce. Soil classification surveys and the like have been conducted by the concerned national agencies. The town's people and some of its history may be encountered in the books of S. Kocagöz, an outspoken and important novelist, and in the writings of authors listed in the book described below. Y. Çagbaylr published in 1989 a rather exhaustive monograph on the town, with the title "Söke," where much space is set aside for the lore and for the public institutions of the county, besides putting together much information which was previously available in scattered form, or not at all.

4. Söke's altitude above sea level is 38 m. The town is situated 37 degrees north latitude, in contrast to 34 for Santa Barbara, 17 for Oaxaca, and 46 for Udine. The hottest month is July with an average temperature of 26.8 degrees Celsius, and August cools to 24.4 (for comparison, Atlanta has 26 degrees C. in August). Annual rainfall of 40 inches in the county is at the upper limit for wheat cultivation and is much greater than for Oaxaca and Santa Barbara. (For comparison, annual precipitation in east central Georgia is 48.6 inches; New York, 42.8 inches; London, 22.9 inches; and San Francisco, 19.7 inches. The Sierra Madre del Sur south of Oaxaca, and the Julian Alps near Udine, have much higher rates of precipitation; and coastal Peru is, of course, rather dry.)

Chapter 4

Constructing the Domestic Assets Scale

This chapter will introduce and discuss the functional areas included in the domestic assets measure and examine the detailed categories of equipment utilized to carry out each function across sample communities. Following examination of the detailed equipment categories, the procedures employed in assigning prices to each item will be examined. The final section will briefly discuss the creation of the domestic assets measure.

Household Functional Areas

As pointed out in chapter 1, early level of living measures consisted of no more than a list of items selected for their ability to differentiate among households with respect to socioeconomic status. Unfortunately, the list was very culturally and time-specific, resulting in a measure of little utility in cross-cultural or longitudinal research. The major innovation of Belcher's functional efficiency approach was to systematize the selection by focusing not on specific items but on household functions. The resulting measure had greater flexibility and utility for a variety of reasons. First, all items that could potentially be used to accomplish a function were included, resulting in a measure that had much greater cross-cultural flexibility. Second, new items can be added as new products or equipment are developed, without automatically necessitating recalibration of the scale.

The domestic assets approach increases the utility of this measure even further by substituting economic value for the questionable ranking of items based on technological efficiency. In addition, this research also seeks to increase the measure's utility by expanding the functional areas that it includes. Indeed, a critical question for this research was, What types of household functions are sufficiently prevalent both within and between societies or cultures to insure the cross-cultural applicability of the measure? Belcher's list of functional areas represented a starting point.

Belcher (1972) used what he termed 14 functional categories of equipment or facilities, but these categories actually assessed only ten different functional dimensions: (1) shelter (assessed by the types of walls, floors, and roofs), (2) potable water supply (assessed in terms of storage and transportation to the home), (3) lighting, (4) food preservation, (5) eating equipment (dishes), (6) human waste disposal, (7) food preparation (assessed in terms of equipment and fuel), (8) floor cleaning equipment, (9) dishwashing, and (10) transportation. This list represented the starting point for this domestic assets study. However, in order to begin with the most encompassing measure possible, a variety of other functional areas were considered. The new list included the ten functional areas mentioned above plus water heating, climate control (heating and cooling), entertainment, communications, food consumption, and bathing.

Thus, the initial working list consisted of 16 potential functional areas, and the next task was to assess their feasibility for cross-cultural research. The evaluations were based on theoretical and practical grounds. On theoretical grounds, certain items were dropped because of their questionable utility in cross-cultural research because of the danger they posed by biasing the measure in favor of some cultural areas over others. For example, in some geographical regions the issue of climate control, whether heating or cooling, was of vital concern, but in other areas it was of little importance. As a result, the inclusion of climate control as a functional area would jeopardize the utility of the domestic assets measure when comparing two different geographical regions; hence, the decision was made to drop this area from the measure.

Practical considerations revolved around the feasibility of developing an exhaustive list of the potential equipment or facilities used to carry out functions and the reliability of information obtained using the categories developed. These much more practical decisions were made during all stages of the research process. The weeding out during the early stages occurred primarily when developing the exhaustive lists of capital goods potentially employed by a household. It quickly became evident that it would be extremely difficult to develop such a scheme for some functional areas. For example, the goods used to serve and consume food border on the infinite, if not in variety, then surely in the possible permutations and combinations displayed within any particular household. Dishes are made from so many different materials and can vary in quality, not only between but within material groupings, that the task seemed insurmountable. Consequently, certain functional areas such as food consumption were dropped early in the process.

Following data collection, it also became evident that the data for some functional areas were of little utility or of questionable reliability because of a failure to anticipate and clearly define the diversity of equipment used. It was realized, of course, that field teams might run into such difficulties. As a result, teams were encouraged to make modifications during the actual data collection by adding more detailed categories with which to code equipment not included in the original instrument. Flexibility had been built into the instrument to allow for this modification. So, if in a particular community an unusual type of technological equipment was used to heat water (a small, wood-burning water heater, for instance), it could easily be incorporated into the interview schedule. Despite these provisions, in some functional areas the diversity of equipment or facilities was simply unanticipated. For example, attempts were made to develop coding categories for component stereo equipment and tape decks. However, feedback from the field and information from the pricing survey strongly suggested that the coding categories and definitions, even with modifications, did not ensure sufficient precision between sample communities. Therefore, the reliability of these items was questionable, and they were subsequently dropped from the final scale. The same was true for the variety of goods used to serve food on such equipment as tables, bars, and other special surfaces.

Also, for practical considerations, the functional area of transportation was dropped. During the planning stages for this research, it was decided to simply record whether or not the household had bicycles, motorcycles, or automobiles. If the household reported any of these items, its make and model would be recorded. Then, published price lists such as blue books would be used to assign a value to each item. Unfortunately, in two sample communities such information was unavailable or difficult to obtain. For that reason, transportation was dropped.

The net result of these theoretical and practical considerations was that the final scale contains domestic assets items reflecting ten functional areas: (1) shelter, (2) food preservation, (3) food preparation, (4) sleeping, (5) human waste disposal, (6) bathing, (7) clothes washing, (8) dish and utensil washing, (9) water heating, and (10) communications. The following sections will deal with the specific procedures used to record and categorize equipment in each of these areas and with the assignment of prices. However, before these specifics can be properly dealt with, two additional issues must be discussed.

These two major issues began to emerge during the development of coding schemes for each functional area. The first issue concerns the number of items to be recorded, and the second focuses on how many different types of equipment within a functional area should be recorded. For example, it is possible that to cook food within a household various types of equipment are used, such as grills, stoves, convection and microwave ovens, toaster ovens, electric skillets, and waffle irons. In these situations the types of food being prepared will determine which type of equipment will be employed, although it is probably safe to say that some types will be used more often than others. Furthermore, it is also possible that a household may have multiple items (for example, two or three electric skillets) within a single category. The issues are (1) how many different types of equipment should be recorded, and then, (2) how many items within a particular type will be recorded.

Utilizing Belcher's *functional efficiency approach*, this was not always an issue because in the case of multiple types of equipment being used for a particular function, the item having the highest functional efficiency rating was always coded. However, with the domestic assets approach, efficiency is not at issue, although an extension of the logic would suggest that only the costliest item should be recorded. Another solution would be to simply record all equipment. But a complete enumeration would be too time-consuming and would greatly jeopardize the possibility of interview completion. After all, how many households, regardless of country, are going to let a stranger into their house to record all of the goods in their possession? The assurance of reliable data collection demanded the development of a truncated list of functional areas with a limited number of items.

The solution adopted in this research to the problems of multiple items and types was handled somewhat differently across functional areas. The consensus was to code, at a minimum, the principal or most often used piece of equipment within a functional area. If feasible given practical constraints, multiple items or types would be coded and included. In certain situations this was less of a problem because the items within a functional area took a Guttman format, that is, if a household reported a particular item, other items would necessarily be present. In these situations, multiple items were again recorded and included in the final measure.

One additional point needs to be made on assigning values to household items. Cost data on all domestic assets, including all of the equipment used to perform domestic functions, were obtained on a *replacement cost* basis. In other words, the value assigned to a particular asset such as a kitchen stove was the current cost of replacing that stove with a similar but new stove. No attempt was made to depreciate the value of items according to their age or physical condition, thereby obtaining a kind of *current market value*, should they be offered for sale. The value used also was not the actual price paid when the item was purchased, but the value of such an item if it were purchased at the time of the survey.

The justification for using replacement cost is associated with the Domestic

Assets Scale's objective when used in disaster and development situations. The argument is that the figures needed are those most closely associated with the cost of reconstruction or reaccumulation of a set of living conditions. In addition, if the focus of the research is development, then the use value, regardless of resale value, is central. In such a situation, the fact that a household has a working refrigerator to insure food preservation is the issue and not the value of the refrigerator in terms of resale. The full logic of this approach will be dealt with more completely in our discussion of shelter (below).

Aside from its theoretical advantages, a simple procedure is needed that can be carried out by interviewers who are neither expert appraisers of household equipment nor professional real estate appraisers. The cost of employing such experts is prohibitive in almost all social science studies where hundreds of households are surveyed; besides, such experts are relatively rare and frequently not available following disasters because of their association with insurance claims. Thus, clear, practical benefits result from employing this procedure.

Detailed Discussion of Functional Areas

The following sections provide a detailed discussion of each functional area and the data collection procedures used. In addition, the actual prices assigned to each type of item will be presented and discussed.

Shelter

One of the major functions usually carried out by a household as a social unit is the provision of shelter. By shelter we refer to the actual structure in which the household resides and carries out many of its activities such as sleeping and cooking. The objective was to obtain a figure that represented the value of the housing unit occupied by a household, if that unit were to be constructed at the time of the interview. This is quite different from the *real estate value* of a dwelling unit since it is not based on *market value*, but on what it would cost to construct a structure of similar quality of the same size at current prices (defined as at the time of the interview). Aside from the fact that the *replacement cost* figure does not represent the *market value* of the dwelling unit, the figure obtained does not include the value of the land on which the unit is constructed.

This logic was used because the nature of the scale relates to disaster and development. The reasoning was that in a disaster, housing units are destroyed and must be replaced, while the land or construction site is usually not destroyed. What is critical is that a structure which provided certain use value to the household has been destroyed. The financial assets, or loss of those assets, is not critical. The significant information needed is the cost to build a new unit of similar size and quality of construction and not the amount of financial loss, as assessed by a real estate market. This means that the housing unit's age and physical condition were not considered in calculating replacement costs, on the assumption that *reconstruction* involves replacement by *new housing* or by repair of damage at current costs.

Another thing to consider in relation to the cost of housing is the unit's ownership. The Domestic Assets Scale assigns the *replacement cost* value of a housing unit to the household occupying the unit regardless of actual ownership. The reasoning is that this scale is not intended to estimate the *net worth* of the household, but to estimate the value of its *living conditions*. A household that rents an expensive house enjoys the *use value* of that dwelling unit and therefore the *living conditions* associated with it. The assignment of house value to a unit's occupant means that the total financial assets of renters are overestimated, and, for some purposes associated with the study of socioeconomic status, a different method may be needed. Accordingly, information was obtained on ownership or tenure status. This makes it theoretically possible to study the accumulation of domestic assets on a basis more like the idea of net worth in that it would allow an evaluation of the domestic assets that a household actually owns. To do this, however, information on indebtedness must be obtained to balance information on accumulated property.

The initial plan in assessing a dwelling structure's economic value had been to obtain a cost figure utilizing a method employed in the Guatemalan Earthquake Study, where detailed information on construction costs with various forms of materials was obtained from architects and builders (Bates 1982). As a result, the interview schedule was designed to obtain detailed information on the structural characteristics of dwellings. These characteristics included the types of materials used to construct the foundation, walls, roofs, and floors of houses as well as information on the type of structure (that is, detached house, row house, apartment building) and on the amount of floor space. Also included was information on services such as plumbing, electrical wiring, and sewage. The intention was to calculate housing values by obtaining information on the construction costs for houses built of various combinations of materials and services. This technique proved unworkable because such data could not be obtained within the project's budget limitations for all six countries. To do so would have required several weeks of expert professional services since such information was not available in published form or in a form easily available to practicing builders and architects. As a consequence, a substitute procedure had to be developed and used.

While it was impossible to use professionals, a number of experts on building costs who were consulted in different countries agreed that reasonably accurate construction cost estimates could be obtained by classifying the housing units into four categories corresponding to *general quality* of construction and by then obtaining figures on construction costs per square meter for these categories. The categories used were as follows:

1. *High-Quality Construction:* Typical of the most expensive housing units in the country, usually occupied by high-income households, and most frequently found in upper-class neighborhoods. Typified by expensive finishing details.

2. *Medium- or Average-Quality Construction:* Typical of middle-class housing occupied by high-status white-collar workers or professionals. Houses made of good materials with good detailing in the medium price range.

3. *Lower-Quality Construction:* Typical of public housing for workers and of private housing used by the working class with lower than middle-class incomes. In poor countries this represented the most frequent type of housing unit. Very plain houses made of inexpensive materials with no frills.

4. *Informal Housing:* Typical of slum dwellings or of self-constructed houses made of salvaged materials obtained virtually without market costs, such as salvaged lumber and bricks, sticks, straw, palm leaves, cane, and other traditional materials.

While these categories imply a systematic categorization across sample communities, such was not the case. In each country the categorization into high, medium, and low was allowed to be sample-specific. In some areas, high quality may imply central electrical wiring and plumbing, while in others central wiring and plumbing are found in all types of structures, with the exception of informal housing. As a result, high-quality construction in one sample community may be very different from high-quality construction in another.

In addition to these categories, the Italian and Yugoslav consultants agreed that construction costs differ between these types of buildings but that by cross-classifying housing units according to quality of construction and type of building, even more reasonable figures per square meter of floor space could be supplied. Accordingly, such figures were obtained from experts in Italy and Yugoslavia and used to estimate the *replacement cost* of housing units. It is probably true that the same procedures could have been employed elsewhere, were such pricing information available. Unfortunately, because of budgetary constraints, such information was not gathered. The additional categories of building types employed in Italy and Yugoslavia were as follows:

1. *Single-Family Dwelling Units:* Includes detached dwellings, duplexes, and row houses of four floors or less.
2. *Multiple-Family Dwelling Units:* Consists of multiple dwelling units higher than four floors.

A modification was made in the Yugoslav case. The initial construction figures obtained were based exclusively on the costs of building materials, without labor costs. As a result, new housing cost figures had to be obtained; by the time new construction costs could be calculated, the Yugoslav economy was involved in a vicious cycle of inflation. Because accurate inflation figures were difficult to obtain, housing costs were adjusted utilizing detailed comparisons of building types and qualities and exchange rate information between the Italian and Yugoslav samples. The assumption was that building quality and type would be closer between the two sample communities in Italy and Yugoslavia than any other possible comparison among the study's sample communities.

The actual value of each household's shelter or dwelling unit for all sample sites was derived in the following two-step procedure. First, construction costs for different quality and (in the Italian and Yugoslav samples) types of structures were obtained from consultants for each sample community. These figures were then applied to each household based on a determination of its quality and type.

The second step, the evaluation of housing quality, was made either by a trained interviewer (in Italy) or based on the status of the sampling sector in which the household unit was located. As discussed in chapter 2, a stratified random sampling technique was employed for each community. A critical component in the sampling scheme was division of the community into clusters of homogeneous housing units. Homogeneity was determined by construction type and quality. It was decided that the sector rating would suffice as a measure of construction quality. The only exception to this procedure was informal housing. Rather than basing costs on sector status, which was always low, individual houses were identified and provided with a separate cost figure. In addition, households in Italy and Yugoslavia were classified as single- or multiple-family dwellings. On the basis of this information, a construction cost figure per square meter was assigned to each household. This figure was then multiplied by the number of square meters within the dwelling unit to arrive at the shelter's final value.

Table 4.1 presents the relative frequencies for building types across samples.

Table 4.1. Households Residing in Specific Types of Dwelling Units (%)

	United States	Italy	Yugoslavia	Mexico	Turkey	Peru
Single house	66.4	20.0	31.4	35.4	19.5	6.1
Duplex	11.1	13.0	6.0	1.4	4.1	3.3
Row house	11.0	5.2	10.7	48.0	25.1	62.9
Compound	0.9	2.6	1.3	5.1	5.7	2.4
Apartment	7.4	57.4	38.8	0.9	28.4	3.3
Apartment in house	2.3	0.4	3.7	3.7	6.5	2.7
Part of apartment	0.0	0.0	2.3	0.3	1.1	1.2
Row of single rooms	0.4	0.4	4.0	1.4	0.5	9.1
Mobile homes	0.4	0.0	1.3	0.0	0.0	0.0
Informal houses	0.0	0.0	0.0	3.1	7.0	8.5
Other	0.0	0.9	0.3	0.6	1.9	0.3
Total	100.0	100.0	100.0	100.0	100.0	100.0
N	239	230	299	350	370	329

Table 4.2. Sample in Each Status Sector (%)

	United States	Italy	Yugoslavia	Mexico	Turkey	Peru
High	16.1	27.4	11.4	23.1	10.1	13.6
Medium	69.3	61.7	36.1	50.6	27.8	45.8
Low	14.6	10.9	52.5	26.3	62.1	40.7
Total	100.0	100.0	100.0	100.0	100.0	100.0
N	239	230	299	350	367	332

These data indicate that single-family dwelling units are the rule in the U.S. sample, and approximately one-third of the households in the Yugoslav and Mexican samples occupy these types of shelters. Apartments are much more the rule in the Italian sample, and row houses dominate the Mexican and Peruvian samples. Informal structures were found in Mexican, Turkish, and Peruvian sample communities; however, in all of these samples they represent fewer than 10 percent of households.

Table 4.2 displays the percentages of households found in each of the different types of sectors. With the exception of the Italian sample, where each

Table 4.3. Construction Costs of Dwelling Units Per Square Meter

Quality	United States All	Italy Single-Family	Italy Multi-family	Yugoslavia Single-Family	Yugoslavia Multi-family	Mexico All	Turkey All	Peru All
High	540	960,000 ($496)	810,000 ($419)	160,000 ($606)	136,000 ($515)	71,890 ($150)	119,700 ($205)	1,495,000 ($130)
Average	432	750,000 ($388)	620,000 ($321)	128,000 ($484)	104,000 ($394)	64,408 ($134)	82,000 ($140)	1,035,000 ($90)
Low	324	600,000 ($310)	500,000 ($259)	84,000 ($319)	72,000 ($273)	64,408 ($134)	40,000 ($68)	632,500 ($55)
Informal	—	—	—	—	—	12,500 ($26)	15,000 ($26)	287,500 ($25)

Monetary values: U.S. dollar, Italian lira, Yugoslav dinar, Mexican peso, Turkish lira, and Peruvian sol.

structure was rated independently, these sector ratings were used to assign construction quality. It must be remembered that informal structures were identified and priced regardless of sector status, which was always identified as low. Again, it is on the basis of the information presented in tables 4.1 and 4.2 that construction costs per square meter were assigned to each household.

The actual construction cost for each type of unit is presented in table 4.3. For comparative purposes, a dollar equivalent figure, based on prevailing exchange rates at the time of data collection, is presented in parentheses. In addition, two figures are presented in the Italian and Yugoslav columns. The first is for single-family dwelling units, and the second for multifamily units. To the extent that these price values are comparable, they indicate that construction costs in the sample communities in the United States, Italy, and Yugoslavia are higher than those for the remaining sample communities. Indeed, the remainder of the sample communities are fairly comparable, although construction prices for the Peruvian sample are consistently lower.

When comparing these cost data, however, it should be remembered that quality is a concept relative to the sample community. As a result, the same quality of housing may include very different types of materials and services such as electrical wiring, plumbing, finishing, or related construction charac-

Table 4.4. Descriptive Statistics on Square Meters of Living Space

	United States	Italy	Yugoslavia	Mexico	Turkey	Peru
Mean	143.6	104.5	72.8	113.0	93.3	126.5
Median	132.0	95.0	70.0	79.0	90.0	80.0

teristics, depending on sample community. These data were used to assign a square meter building cost for each household; this figure was subsequently multiplied by the number of square meters of living space in each dwelling unit.

The data in table 4.4 suggest considerable variability in typical living spaces across sampling communities. Focusing on median values, which better capture the typical household, given the skewed distributions found in some countries, the highest value per square meters of living space is found in the U.S. sample, followed, in order, by Italy, Turkey, Peru, Mexico, and Yugoslavia.

In subsequent sections dealing with specific functional areas and their associated equipment, descriptive statistics for total value will be of little utility. However, in the case of shelter, these statistics may provide additional understanding of the procedure being employed and the basic comparability we are seeking through use of the domestic assets measure. Therefore, table 4.5 presents the mean and median values for shelter, expressed both in sample-specific currency values and in exchange dollars. Again, given the positive skewness that occurs in each sample, it makes more sense to utilize median values in assessing the typical value of shelter across samples. As one might expect, the value of shelter in the sample communities of high-income nations is priced considerably higher than those located in low-income nations.

It is important to remember that these values represent building costs of the dwelling unit at the time of the interview and not necessarily real estate value. In addition, the value of plumbing and wiring has been included implicitly in the construction values, when these items are normally associated with construction techniques. As a consequence, in some samples even the lowest-quality housing includes centralized electrical wiring and complete plumbing, while in other samples it may include only limited wiring and no plumbing. This in part accounts for the variations seen in housing costs per square meter and the variations we find across samples. Thus, while the domestic assets measure does not explicitly include these items, in some areas they are indirectly subsumed in the costs of construction.

Table 4.5. Descriptive Statistics for Value of Shelter

Location	National Currency	Exchange ($)
United States		
Mean	65,335	65,335
Median	57,024	57,024
Italy		
Mean	71,730,045	37,089
Median	64,800,000	33,506
Yugoslavia		
Mean	7,445,876	25,326
Median	6,396,000	21,755
Mexico		
Mean	7,323,517	15,257
Median	4,830,600	10,063
Turkey		
Mean	5,431,869	9,301
Median	3,960,000	6,780
Peru		
Mean	115,612,685	10,053
Median	72,450,000	6,300

Food Preservation

A series of questions was asked of the principal respondent to determine types of equipment utilized to store food that can become spoiled. These questions were designed to determine: (1) if a refrigerator or some other form of equipment was being used; (2) if a refrigerator was used, then a series of questions determined the type and number of refrigerators in use; and (3) a supplemental question was asked to determine whether some form of free-standing freezer was in use.

Table 4.6 presents the relative frequencies of different types of food preservation equipment utilized across samples. Examination of the table suggests that the vast majority of households in the U.S. and Italian samples use some kind of refrigerator. The same holds for other samples; however, significantly higher percentages of households utilize something other than refrigerators. In fact, in the Yugoslav, Turkish, Peruvian, and Mexican samples, respectively, 6, 11.6, 33.7, and 34.5 percent of the households use something other than refrigerators to preserve food. Perhaps most interesting is the fact that almost

Table 4.6. Households with Specific Food Preservation Equipment (%)

	United States	Italy	Yugoslavia	Mexico	Turkey	Peru
Refrigerators						
Side-by-side, ice and water	16.3	0.0	0.0	0.3	0.0	0.0
Side-by-side, ice	3.8	0.4	0.0	0.0	1.4	0.0
Side-by-side	8.3	0.0	0.0	0.3	0.3	0.3
Large, ice and water	2.4	0.0	0.0	0.6	0.0	0.0
Large, ice	11.8	14.4	0.0	0.3	10.0	0.3
Large	30.2	3.9	3.7	4.9	7.6	9.3
Midsize	21.1	53.7	30.5	49.9	61.6	47.9
Compact	2.9	24.0	46.3	6.3	5.9	7.5
Other items						
Icebox	0.0	0.0	0.7	0.0	0.0	0.0
Spring house	0.0	0.4	0.3	0.0	0.8	0.0
Plastic/metal ice chest	0.4	0.0	0.3	0.6	0.0	0.3
Styrofoam ice chest	0.0	0.0	0.0	0.3	0.0	0.3
Food cabinet	0.0	0.0	0.0	3.2	1.9	2.7
Boxes	0.0	0.0	0.0	4.0	1.9	6.6
Nothing	0.0	0.0	4.7	26.4	7.0	23.8
Refrigerator combinations						
2 side-by-side	1.0	0.0	0.0	0.0	0.0	0.0
Side-by-side and large	1.4	0.0	0.0	0.3	0.0	0.0
Side-by-side, 1 large, 2 midsize	0.0	0.0	0.0	0.3	0.0	0.0
Side-by-side, midsize	0.0	0.0	0.0	0.3	0.0	0.0
2 large	0.5	0.9	0.7	0.0	0.0	0.0
Large and midsize	0.0	0.4	2.0	0.3	0.3	0.3
Large and compact	0.0	0.0	0.3	0.0	0.0	0.0
Large, midsize, and compact	0.0	0.0	0.3	0.0	0.0	0.0
2 midsize	0.0	0.4	2.3	1.1	1.1	0.6
Midsize, compact	0.0	0.4	7.0	0.6	0.3	0.0
2 compacts	0.0	0.9	0.7	0.3	0.0	0.0
Total*	100.0	100.0	100.0	100.0	100.0	100.0
N	239	229	298	349	370	332
Freezers						
Large	17.7	7.4	9.7	0.6	0.8	0.6
Small	5.7	29.3	44.7	0.6	0.5	0.9

Table 4.6. *(Continued)*

	United States	Italy	Yugoslavia	Mexico	Turkey	Peru
None	76.6	63.3	45.7	98.8	98.6	98.5
Total*	100.0	100.0	100.0	100.0	100.0	100.0
N	239	229	300	350	370	332

*May not total 100.0 because of rounding.

one-fourth of households in the Mexican and Peruvian samples utilize no special equipment to preserve food. These figures could be slightly higher when we consider that many of the other items used, such as boxes and food cabinets, offer very limited means of food preservation.

The above information was incorporated into the domestic assets measure by first determining the type of equipment used by a household and then by assigning the current market value of this item to the household. In cases where multiple types of equipment are employed, their prices were simply combined. In other words, if the household reported two compact refrigerators, they received double the value of a compact refrigerator in their total domestic assets score. It must be remembered that the actual cost of these individual equipment types was obtained by an independent market survey. As can clearly be seen, the item categories associated with food preservation equipment are sufficiently detailed to allow for reliable pricing. Presented in table 4.7 are the actual prices utilized.

Some potential problems with these data should be kept in mind. First, while provision was made for the possibility of recording multiple refrigerators, the same does not hold for other types of food preservation equipment. Second, should a household report some form of refrigerator, the possibility of recording other types of food preservation equipment was not allowed for. In other words, it is very likely that households having refrigerators also have cabinets or ice chests; however, because of coding limitations this information was not obtained. The net effects of these two problems in reporting on equipment used to preserve food are difficult to gauge. It may be safe to suggest that these net effects roughly cancel each other out. That is, failing to record multiple non-refrigerator items for households that have or do not have refrigerators may result in an overall attenuation of the contributions of food preservation for the

Table 4.7. Prices Assigned to Specific Food Preservation Equipment

	United States	Italy	Yugoslavia	Mexico	Turkey	Peru
Refrigerators						
Side-by-side, ice and water	1,225	4,500,000*	—	—	467,200	30,160,000*
Side-by-side, ice	800	—	—	—	408,800	—
Side-by-side	700	1,225,000	—	216,349*	—	—
Large, ice and water	1,000	—	—	—	—	—
Large, ice	785	778,000	—	—	—	—
Large	620	750,000	271,180	150,098†	224,000†	8,050,000†
Midsize	550	679,500	223,445	109,040	175,000	3,470,000
Compact	205	397,000	132,640	89,311	96,000	2,490,000
Other items						
Plastic/metal ice chest	50	30,000	2,645	14,500	28,500	575,000
Styrofoam ice chest	4	—	—	2,400	—	115,000
Icebox	—	—	7,936‡	—	—	—
Food cabinet	—	—	1,885	23,675	—	—
Boxes/spring house	0	0	0	0	—	0
Large freezer	470	450,000	241,050	123,700	274,480	11,810,000
Small freezer	250	446,000	144,382	93,100	146,000	—

*Price used on all side-by-side refrigerators.
†Price used on all large refrigerators.
‡Price is three times the price of an ice chest.

total measure, but it does not systematically bias one type of household over another. ,

Food Preparation

Food preparation equipment represents one of the most difficult functional areas to assess because of the widely varied types of equipment used by households, and each household also may use a multitude of different items. Our decision was not to capture the possible variety of equipment used, but rather to focus on primary food preparation equipment. The principal respondent was first asked what piece of equipment most often was used to cook food. If the response was some type of gas or electric cooking appliance, then a series of questions was asked that was designed to determine whether it was a range or some component system. Additional information such as the size, types of cleaning features, number and types of ovens, the fuel used, and stove design was also obtained.

The data on cooking equipment are presented in table 4.8. Examination of these data indicates that the majority of households in the U.S., Italian, Yugoslav, and Mexican samples used some form of cooking range consisting of a stove and oven(s). The Santa Barbara sample appears to have the greatest diversity, displaying a wide variety of ranges as well as component systems. The households within other sample sites display much greater homogeneity. However, these data underreport the diversity displayed among compact ranges in Italy. Indeed, size seems to have little relevance to price in Italy, where all ranges tend to be small but display a great variety of options. The Turkish and Peruvian data display a much greater relative number of households using something other than ranges, and many households depend on countertop gas or kerosene stoves. Again, it must be remembered that the nature of the questions asked were such that they captured only the principal types of equipment utilized in food preparation. It is possible, and probably certain, that a much wider variety of equipment is used to prepare food in every country.

Table 4.9 presents the price attached to each type of food preparation equipment for each sample community. Not every combination of items is listed, as is the case with component systems. Where some form of component system was used, the individual components were priced and then combined to obtain the value of the particular types of equipment employed. It also must be reported that in some situations prices for particular items were not obtained through the pricing survey; instead, prices for similar items were substituted, sometimes in an adjusted form, to approximate the actual cost.

Table 4.8. Households with Specific Food Preparation Equipment (%)

	United States	Italy	Yugoslavia	Mexico	Turkey	Peru
Full-size ranges						
Double ovens						
Microwave-convection						
Self-cleaning	2.5	0.0	0.0	0.0	0.0	0.0
Continuous cleaning	2.9	0.0	0.0	0.3	0.0	0.0
No cleaning feature	0.0	0.0	2.0	0.0	0.0	0.0
Convection						
Self-cleaning	8.4	0.4	0.7	0.0	0.3	0.0
Continuous cleaning	0.0	0.0	0.0	0.0	0.0	0.0
No cleaning feature	3.4	0.0	2.0	0.6	4.4	0.0
Single ovens						
Self-cleaning	8.1	4.4	5.1	0.0	0.3	0.0
Continuous cleaning	0.5	1.3	0.0	0.0	0.3	0.6
No cleaning feature	39.1	34.4	69.6	35.7	19.6	7.3
Compact ranges						
Self-cleaning	0.0	5.3	0.0	0.0	0.3	0.0
Continuous cleaning	0.0	2.2	0.0	0.0	0.0	2.4
No cleaning feature	2.6	49.3	4.1	44.9	6.8	30.7
*Separates**						
Double wall ovens						
Microwave-convection						
Self-cleaning	1.5	0.0	0.0	0.0	0.0	0.0
Continuous cleaning	8.0	0.0	0.3	0.0	0.0	0.0
No cleaning feature	0.0	0.0	0.3	0.3	0.0	0.0
Convection						
Self-cleaning	5.9	0.0	0.0	0.3	0.0	0.0
Continuous cleaning	3.1	0.0	0.0	0.0	0.3	0.0
No cleaning feature	0.9	0.0	0.0	0.0	0.5	0.0
Single wall ovens						
Self-cleaning	1.5	0.4	0.3	0.0	0.0	0.0
Continuous cleaning	2.0	0.0	0.0	0.0	0.0	0.0
No cleaning feature	6.6	1.8	2.4	0.6	1.6	1.2
Other food preparation equipment						
Countertop gas stove	0.0	0.4	1.4	6.1	44.8	0.0
Countertop kerosene stove	0.0	0.0	0.0	3.5	0.8	0.0

Table 4.8. *(Continued)*

	United States	Italy	Yugoslavia	Mexico	Turkey	Peru
Kerosene stove and oven	0.0	0.0	0.3	0.3	1.4	35.6
Electric hot plate	2.6	0.0	4.4	2.3	12.8	1.2
Toaster oven	0.0	0.0	0.7	0.0	0.0	11.9
Iron stove and oven	0.0	0.0	5.7	0.0	0.0	0.0
Iron stove	0.0	0.0	0.3	0.0	0.5	0.0
Clay stove and oven	0.0	0.0	0.3	0.0	0.0	0.0
Charcoal burning grill	0.4	0.0	0.0	2.6	0.0	0.0
Open fire	0.0	0.0	0.0	2.0	0.0	8.8
Other	0.0	0.0	0.0	0.6	5.4	0.0
No cooking equipment	0.0	0.0	0.0	0.0	0.0	0.3
Total[†]	100.0	100.0	100.0	100.0	100.0	100.0
N	234	227	296	345	368	329

*Plus a cooktop.
[†]May not total 100.0 because of rounding.

'able 4.9. Prices Assigned to Specific Food Preparation Equipment

	United States	Italy	Yugoslavia	Mexico	Turkey	Peru
ull-size ranges						
ingle-ovens	518	466,250	72,880*	62,635*	145,500*	8,135,750
Self-cleaning	655	534,000	—	—	—	10,981,500
Continuous cleaning	560	534,000	—	—	—	8,000,000
No cleaning feature	380	398,500	—	—	—	5,290,000
)ouble-ovens						
Self-cleaning	960	—	—	—	—	—
Continuous cleaning	670	—	—	—	—	—
No cleaning feature	630	—	76,450[†]	—	—	—
Microwave-convection						
Self-cleaning	1,030	—	—	—	—	—
Continuous cleaning	935	—	—	—	—	—
No cleaning feature	—	—	—	—	—	—

Table 4.9. *(Continued)*

	United States	Italy	Yugoslavia	Mexico	Turkey	Peru
Compact ranges						
Self-cleaning	—	526,000‡	—	—	—	—
No cleaning feature	300	331,500	49,398	57,919	92,000§	2,252,500
Wall ovens						
Single						
General	463	—	51,375‖	—	—	6,400,000
Self-cleaning	555	—	—	—	—	—
Continuous cleaning	380	—	—	—	—	—
No cleaning feature	370	—	—	—	—	—
Double						
General	628	—	68,500	—	—	—
Self-cleaning	775	—	—	—	—	—
Continuous cleaning	480	—	—	—	—	—
Microwave	375	565,000	—	—	650,000	7,137,500
Regular cooktop	225	—	67,947	—	—	3,300,000
Smooth cooktop	370	—	—	—	—	—
Other cooking equipment						
Electric hot plate	38	—	9,486	4,750	16,000	219,000
Toaster oven	50	103,620	—	—	47,000	575,000
Charcoal grill	43	—	—	—	—	—
Kerosene stove/oven	—	—	—	—	30,000	754,800
Kerosene oven	—	—	26,648	—	—	—
Iron stove/oven	—	—	24,414	—	30,000	—
Iron stove	—	—	18,440	—	—	—
Clay stove	—	—	12,207#	—	—	—

* Price used for all single oven ranges.
† Price used for all double oven ranges.
‡ Price used for all compact ranges with cleaning features.
§ Price used for all compact ranges.
‖ Price is 75 percent of the price of a double oven.
Price is 50 percent of the price of an iron stove.

Table 4.10. Households with Specific Clothes Washing Equipment (%)

	United States	Italy	Yugoslavia	Mexico	Turkey	Peru
Automatic washer and dryer	53.2	2.2	8.0	0.3	2.2	0.6
Automatic washer	10.4	92.2	61.7	8.0	5.7	7.3
Semiautomatic washer	0.4	3.5	5.7	3.2	25.4	6.4
Manual washer	0.0	0.0	5.0	21.5	10.3	3.0
Special basin (e.g., *pila*)	0.0	1.3	8.0	65.9	1.9	29.5
Washpan or tub	0.0	0.0	7.7	0.6	45.9	48.0
No special equipment	36.0	0.9	4.0	0.6	8.4	3.3
Other	0.0	0.0	0.0	0.0	0.3	1.8
Total*	100.0	100.0	100.0	100.0	100.0	100.0
N	239	230	300	349	370	329

*May not total 100.0 because of rounding.

Clothes Washing

A single question was asked about how the household's clothing was washed. Table 4.10 presents the responses. Examination of the relative frequencies suggests that substantial proportions of households in the U.S., Italian, and Yugoslav samples have automatic washing machines, while households in the Mexican, Turkish, and Peruvian samples use more labor-intensive equipment. However, it is interesting that a large proportion of households in the U.S. sample use no special equipment. Instead, clothing is taken to laundromats or to laundry and dry cleaning services. The households having no special equipment in Peru are more likely to have their clothing washed by other households that perform such services to earn additional income. The prices attached to each type of clothes washing equipment are presented in table 4.11. Those households that had no special equipment received zero weight.

Dishwashing

The equipment used by a household to wash dishes and cooking utensils was also assessed by a single question. The relative frequencies of different types of dishwashing equipment are presented in table 4.12. As might be expected, a large proportion of the households in both the U.S. and Italian samples use

**Table 4.11. Prices Assigned to Specific Clothes Washing
and Clothes Drying Equipment**

	United States	Italy	Yugoslavia	Mexico	Turkey	Peru
Washpan or tub	10	—	1,162	1,538	600	30,500
Special utility sink	59	141,800	16,395	15,442	2,000	408,700
Manual washer	—	—	—	41,553	40,000	1,666,900
Semiautomatic washer	400	—	—	57,320	135,000	1,666,900
Automatic washer	390	701,300*	64,100*	93,921	223,000	9,323,000
Automatic dryer	300	400,000	46,480	119,048	175,200	8,960,000

*Price also used for semiautomatic and manual washers where necessary.

**Table 4.12. Households with Specific Dishwashing Equipment
or Facilities (%)**

	United States	Italy	Yugoslavia	Mexico	Turkey	Peru
Electric dishwasher	71.4	32.8	0.0	3.0	0.3	0.5
Kitchen sink	28.6	66.8	51.0	93.6	36.2	75.7
Cement sink	0.0	0.0	35.2	0.3	24.4	4.6
Dishpan	0.0	0.0	13.5	2.7	37.2	18.4
Public fountain	0.0	0.4	0.0	0.3	0.0	0.0
River/lake	0.0	0.0	0.0	0.0	0.6	0.0
Other	0.0	0.0	0.3	0.0	1.2	0.8
Total*	100.0	100.0	100.0	100.0	100.0	100.0
N	239	229	349	299	320	370

*May not total 100.0 because of rounding.

automatic dishwashers, while substantially larger portions of the households
in other samples use some form of kitchen sink. The prices attached to each
form of equipment are presented in table 4.13. If a household reported the use
of automatic dishwashers, they received the value of a dishwasher and a sink,
since in most situations a sink is also used in washing activities. Of course, it
is possible that a household with dishwashers or even kitchen sinks has other
types of dishwashing equipment that are used from time to time. However,

Table 4.13. Prices Assigned to Specific Dishwashing Equipment

	United States	Italy	Yugoslavia	Mexico	Turkey	Peru
Electric dishwasher	430	524,000	89,550	90,499	407,000	4,945,000
Kitchen sink	215	91,500	15,072*	12,367*	137,300	817,400
Cement sink	59	—	—	—	2,000	408,700
Dishpan	10	—	5,617	500	1,150	15,250
Public fountain	0	0	0	0	0	0
River/lake	0	0	0	0	0	0

*Price also assigned to cement sink.

it does not necessarily follow that all households have additional equipment. Therefore, the values of other types of equipment were not added.

Water Heating

As with dishwashing equipment, information about equipment used to heat water was obtained using a single question. The data are presented in table 4.14. The majority of households in the U.S., Italian, and Yugoslav samples employ either an automatic water heater with tank or a central boiler system. Substantial proportions of the households in the Mexican and Peruvian samples have no special equipment for heating water. At first glance, the large proportions of households having no equipment to heat water may appear to introduce bias into the domestic assets measure. However, it is evident that given sufficient disposable income, even in these countries, households will purchase water heating equipment. Therefore, this item is a legitimate addition because of the apparent prevalence of expectations toward heating water for household use.

The prices assigned to water heating equipment are presented in table 4.15. Households indicating that they heat water using their stove or fireplace did not receive any additional value to their domestic assets measure because in most cases these items were also used for food preparation. (Since the value of this equipment was included when evaluating food preparation, it was not added here.) Households reporting a central boiler system had the value of an automatic water heater added to their domestic assets measure. Households reporting no special equipment were given the value of zero, and households reporting other, unspecified equipment were dropped from the analysis.

Table 4.14. Households with Specific Water Heating Equipment (%)

	United States	Italy	Yugoslavia	Mexico	Turkey	Peru
Modern solar	4.3	0.0	0.0	0.0	0.0	0.0
Automatic with tank	95.3	61.7	35.1	12.9	1.9	1.8
Manual with tank	0.0	8.7	9.7	18.9	41.2	6.7
Manual on pipe	0.0	5.7	18.1	18.8	29.2	4.9
Central boiler	0.4	17.8	20.1	0.0	1.1	0.0
Tank on roof	0.0	0.0	0.0	0.6	1.1	0.3
Fire or stove	0.0	3.0	13.4	16.6	24.4	27.7
No special equipment	0.0	2.2	3.3	32.0	1.1	58.3
Other	0.0	0.0	0.3	0.0	0.0	0.3
Total*	100.0	100.0	100.0	100.0	100.0	100.0
N	239	230	299	350	369	328

*May not total 100.0 because of rounding.

Table 4.15. Prices Assigned to Specific Water Heating Equipment

	United States	Italy	Yugoslavia	Mexico	Turkey	Peru
Modern solar	600	—	—	—	—	—
Automatic with tank	190	161,250	39,341	23,536	130,000	464,500
Manual with tank	—	80,625	19,671*	11,768*	75,000	232,250*
Manual on pipe	—	190,750	10,263	11,768*	75,000	232,250*
Central boiler	190†	161,250†	39,341†	23,536†	—	464,500†
Tank on roof	—	—	—	15,534‡	85,800‡	306,570‡
Fire or stove	0	0	0	0	0	0
No special equipment	0	0	0	0	0	0

*Price is 50 percent of the price of an automatic with tank.
†Price is the same as the price of an automatic with tank.
‡Price is 66 percent of the price of an automatic with tank.

Table 4.16. Households with Specific Bathing Facilities (%)

	United States	Italy	Yugoslavia	Mexico	Turkey	Peru
Tub or shower	98.5	95.7	69.7	52.0	57.6	44.7
Outside tub	0.0	2.2	14.3	5.5	3.3	5.5
Shared tub	0.0	0.9	3.7	3.4	0.0	15.9
Sink or basin	0.0	0.0	10.0	0.3	9.8	1.5
Special pan	1.5	0.9	1.7	38.2	21.7	27.8
River/lake	0.0	0.0	0.3	0.0	0.0	1.8
Other	0.0	0.4	0.3	0.6	7.6	2.8
Total*	100.0	100.0	100.0	100.0	100.0	100.0
N	239	230	300	348	368	327

*May not total 100.0 because of rounding.

Bathing

The data on bathing facilities for each sample are presented in table 4.16. These data suggest that the majority of households in all sample communities utilize either a tub or shower for bathing. There is some variation as to whether the tub/shower is inside the dwelling unit or shared with other households. In addition, a substantial proportion of households in the Peruvian, Turkish, and Mexican samples do not use tubs or showers but some form of special pans.

The pricing of bathing equipment was somewhat more difficult than other items because the information collected did not differentiate between tubs and showers. As a result, prices for tubs, which were generally more expensive than showers, were used. This will inflate the contribution of this item in sample communities where showers are the rule. After determining the type of equipment, price assignment was straightforward, with the exception of shared tubs/showers. In the event that the household shared a tub or shower, they simply received half of the value of a tub/shower; those households reporting an outside facility simply received the value of a tub/shower. In addition, information on the number of tubs/showers owned by the household was collected and included in the pricing through simple multiplication of appropriate value by this number. Data on the number of tubs/showers found in households across sample communities are presented in table 4.17, and the prices assigned to each type of equipment employed by a household are presented in table 4.18.

Table 4.17. Households with Specific Number of Bathing Facilities (%)

	United States	Italy	Yugoslavia	Mexico	Turkey	Peru
1	42.2	75.3	88.8	63.5	98.2	67.1
2	42.1	20.7	10.4	29.6	1.3	23.0
3	10.6	3.5	0.4	4.9	0.4	8.1
4	4.1	0.4	0.4	2.0	—	0.9
5	0.9	—	—	—	—	0.9
Total*	100.0	100.0	100.0	100.0	100.0	100.0
N	239	227	203	249	222	225

*May not total 100.0 because of rounding.

Table 4.18. Prices Assigned to Bathing Facilities

	United States	Italy	Yugoslavia	Mexico	Turkey	Peru
Tub or shower	150	260,500	97,111	10,725,000	53,500	1,725,000
Sink or basin	137	146,100	15,072	48,966	27,750	862,500
Special pan	—	16,496	1,162	1,538	1,150	15,250
River/lake	0	0	0	0	0	0

Human Waste Disposal

The data concerning human waste disposal for all samples are presented in table 4.19. These data indicate that the majority of households across all samples used toilets attached to community sewage systems or some form of septic system. A relatively large proportion of the households in the Yugoslav, Mexican, Turkish, and Peruvian samples, however, employ outhouses or latrines where in most cases the waste falls into a simple pit. In other words, no form of waste treatment system is used by the household.

The pricing of these facilities was handled in a manner similar to bathing facilities. The specific prices are presented in table 4.20. Pricing information on outhouses or latrines was difficult to obtain; therefore, the solution adopted was simply to assign half the value of a toilet to these households. In addition, information on the number of toilets owned by the household was obtained

Table 4.19. Households with Specific Human Waste Disposal Equipment (%)

	United States	Italy	Yugoslavia	Mexico	Turkey	Peru
Flush toilet	100.0	99.6	71.0	58.3	48.4	57.8
Latrine	0.0	0.0	19.7	14.9	28.6	1.8
Outhouse	0.0	0.0	5.7	19.8	17.3	28.6
Public	0.0	0.4	1.3	4.6	2.7	2.1
None	0.0	0.0	1.7	2.0	0.5	8.8
Other	0.0	0.0	0.7	0.3	2.4	0.9
Total*	100.0	100.0	100.0	100.0	100.0	100.0
N	239	229	300	348	370	329

*May not total 100.0 because of rounding.

Table 4.20. Prices Assigned to Specific Human Waste Disposal Equipment

	United States	Italy	Yugoslavia	Mexico	Turkey	Peru
Flush toilet	189	165,250	70,212	81,792	29,750	550,000
Latrine/outhouse	—	—	35,106	40,896	14,875	275,000*
None	0	0	0	0	0	0

*Price is 50 percent of the price of a flush toilet.

and included by simply multiplying the value assigned to the household by the appropriate number. The data on the number of toilets across all samples are presented in table 4.21.

Sleeping Facilities

Since a large number of households consist of more than a single individual, and as the number of individuals increases, the type and number of beds will increase, information on facilities was collected so that two different types of sleeping equipment (beds) could be recorded along with the number of each

Table 4.21. Households with Specific Number of Toilets (%)

	United States	Italy	Yugoslavia	Mexico	Turkey	Peru
1	22.9	75.4	83.7	60.6	71.7	65.0
2	49.1	21.5	15.0	27.1	26.0	23.2
3	21.0	3.1	0.9	8.1	1.2	8.8
4	5.6	—	0.4	2.3	1.2	2.0
5	1.4	—	—	1.8	—	1.0
Total*	100.0	100.0	100.0	100.0	100.0	100.0
N	239	229	300	348	370	329

*May not total 100.0 because of rounding.

type. The data for sleeping facilities are presented in table 4.22, which has been divided into two sections. The upper section indicates the principal type of sleeping item employed, and the lower section presents the secondary item. Examination of these data suggests that a greater variety of types of equipment are employed in Mexico and Turkey than in other sample communities. Table 4.23 presents the number of primary and secondary items found in households reporting some form of equipment for each sample.

The prices assigned to each type of sleeping equipment are presented in table 4.24. The total figure for each household was obtained by multiplying the value of each type of bed by the number of each type and then summing these values to create a single figure that indicated the total value of sleeping equipment employed by the household.

Communications

The final functional area included in the domestic assets measure deals with communications. In modern societies with their highly differentiated structures and geographically dispersed populations, communication between a household and its surrounding community and society becomes increasingly important. Therefore, a series of questions was asked of each household to determine the variety of equipment employed by the household in carrying out this function. In particular, information was obtained on whether the household possessed phones, radios, and televisions. Television sets also were divided into color and black and white. In addition, the number of each type of equipment was obtained. The data are presented in table 4.25.

Table 4.22. Households with Specific Sleeping Facilities (%)

	United States	Italy	Yugoslavia	Mexico	Turkey	Peru
Primary						
King/Queen	53.5	52.6	39.5	22.5	1.9	10.3
Full/Twin	45.2	40.0	19.1	70.9	18.4	73.8
Hideaway bed	1.3	0.0	15.1	0.0	2.2	0.3
Studio/bunk	0.0	7.0	0.7	0.0	5.9	14.0
Couch	0.0	0.0	19.4	0.0	47.0	0.0
Folding bed	0.0	0.4	6.0	1.2	5.9	0.0
Cot	0.0	0.0	0.0	1.2	1.9	1.5
Pad or mat	0.0	0.0	0.0	2.3	1.1	0.0
Floor	0.0	0.0	0.0	0.3	2.7	0.0
Mat on metal strips	0.0	0.0	0.0	0.0	13.0	0.0
Other	0.0	0.0	0.3	1.7	0.0	0.0
Total*	100.0	100.0	100.0	100.0	100.0	100.0
N	239	230	299	347	370	329
Secondary						
King/Queen	2.5	1.7	2.9	1.1	3.1	3.7
Full/Twin	68.4	4.5	4.0	26.4	11.0	83.3
Hideaway bed	25.8	0.0	17.2	6.2	1.3	0.6
Studio/bunk	2.7	89.4	1.7	2.2	4.8	10.5
Couch	0.7	1.7	60.3	0.6	37.0	0.0
Folding bed	0.0	1.1	12.6	21.9	4.4	1.9
Cot	0.0	1.7	0.0	8.4	4.0	0.0
Pad or mat	0.0	0.0	0.0	16.3	2.2	0.0
Floor	0.0	0.0	0.0	0.6	9.3	0.0
Mat on metal strips	0.0	0.0	0.0	0.0	22.9	0.0
Other	0.0	0.0	0.6	16.3	0.0	0.0
Total*	100.0	100.0	100.0	100.0	100.0	100.0
N	146	179	174	178	227	162

*May not total 100.0 because of rounding.

Table 4.23. Households with Specific Number of Primary and Secondary Sleeping Facilities (%)

	United States	Italy	Yugoslavia	Mexico	Turkey	Peru
Primary						
1	42.2	90.9	80.5	16.0	27.3	33.1
2	28.9	4.8	14.8	29.4	30.0	19.5
3	23.8	1.7	4.0	21.6	19.5	19.8
4	2.8	1.3	0.0	16.0	12.4	10.9
5	1.9	0.0	0.7	8.7	5.1	6.7
6	0.5	0.9	0.0	3.8	2.2	4.9
7	0.0	0.4	0.0	1.5	2.4	2.4
8	0.0	0.0	0.0	2.0	0.3	2.1
9	0.0	0.0	0.0	0.9	0.0	0.6
10	0.0	0.0	0.0	0.0	0.0	0.0
Total*	100.0	100.0	100.0	100.0	100.0	100.0
N	239	230	298	343	370	329
Secondary						
1	36.3	40.4	61.4	57.6	43.8	39.5
2	32.2	47.8	25.1	27.1	32.6	27.2
3	24.0	9.6	8.2	9.6	16.1	15.4
4	6.8	1.1	4.1	3.4	2.7	9.9
5	0.7	1.1	1.2	0.0	2.7	2.5
6	0.0	0.0	0.0	1.1	1.8	1.2
7	0.0	0.0	0.0	0.0	0.4	1.9
8	0.0	0.0	0.0	0.6	0.0	1.2
9	0.0	0.0	0.0	0.6	0.0	1.2
10	0.0	0.0	0.0	0.0	0.0	0.0
Total*	100.0	100.0	100.0	100.0	100.0	100.0
N	146	178	171	177	224	162

*May not total 100.0 because of rounding.

Table 4.24. Prices Assigned to Specific Sleeping Facilities

	United States	Italy	Yugoslavia	Mexico	Turkey	Peru
King/Queen	695	1,321,000	36,352	45,847	225,000	1,335,000
Full/Twin	389	339,000	21,229	37,873	112,500	1,335,000
Hideaway bed	330	1,756,500	37,530	96,625	125,000	3,384,500
Studio/bunk	330	688,000	28,305	14,500	85,000	814,500
Couch	—	688,000	38,550	53,000	85,000	—
Folding bed	100	116,700	21,700	12,700	19,500	814,500
Cot	40	52,700	—	6,150	9,900	180,000
Pad or mat	—	—	—	5,247	2,750	—
Floor	0	0	0	0	0	0
Mat on metal strips	—	0	—	—	7,000	0

Table 4.25. Households with Specific Communication Equipment (%)

	United States	Italy	Yugoslavia	Mexico	Turkey	Peru
Telephone						
0	2.9	6.6	50.0	69.2	74.1	92.2
1	27.0	80.7	48.3	28.5	25.4	7.5
2	37.6	11.0	1.3	1.7	0.5	0.0
3	24.5	1.8	0.3	0.3	0.0	0.3
4	2.3	0.0	0.0	0.3	0.0	0.0
5	3.8	0.0	0.0	0.0	0.0	0.0
6	0.5	0.0	0.0	0.0	0.0	0.0
7	1.4	0.0	0.0	0.0	0.0	0.0
Total*	100.0	100.0	100.0	100.0	100.0	100.0
N	239	228	300	347	370	332
Radio						
0	0.4	2.6	9.3	9.5	20.0	12.5
1	30.2	57.5	81.7	69.5	74.1	79.0
2	36.9	22.4	5.7	14.7	4.9	4.3
3	17.6	12.3	2.3	4.0	0.8	2.7
4	12.6	2.6	0.3	1.7	0.3	0.9

Table 4.25. *(Continued)*

	United States	Italy	Yugoslavia	Mexico	Turkey	Peru
5	2.3	2.2	0.7	0.6	0.0	0.6
6	0.0	0.4	0.0	0.0	0.0	0.0
Total*	100.0	100.0	100.0	100.0	100.0	100.0
N	239	228	300	347	370	329
Black and white TV						
0	68.7	57.8	40.1	24.0	28.7	33.1
1	30.9	39.6	57.0	66.3	69.9	65.4
2	0.5	1.3	2.6	8.6	1.4	1.2
3	0.0	1.3	0.3	0.6	0.0	0.3
4	0.0	0.0	0.0	0.6	0.0	0.0
Total*	100.0	100.0	100.0	100.0	100.0	100.0
N	239	230	300	350	370	332
Color TV						
0	4.2	26.1	50.0	77.7	71.6	76.7
1	62.7	70.9	47.7	20.0	26.8	22.2
2	24.1	2.6	2.3	2.3	1.6	1.1
3	7.1	0.4	0.0	0.0	0.0	0.0
4	1.8	0.0	0.0	0.0	0.0	0.0
Total*	100.0	100.0	100.0	100.0	100.0	100.0
N	238	229	300	350	370	332

*May not total 100.0 because of rounding.

Examination of these data reveals a number of interesting findings. In the U.S. and Italian samples the vast majority of households report telephones, and exactly half of the Yugoslav households report them. Slightly more than one-fourth of the households in the Mexican and Turkish samples report telephones, while only 7.5 percent of the Peruvian households do so. A very different picture emerges when the percentages of households with radios and televisions are examined. Indeed, the vast majority of households across all samples re-

able 4.26. Prices Assigned to Specific Communication Equipment

	United States	Italy	Yugoslavia	Mexico	Turkey	Peru
elephone	40	62,400	16,112	19,637	7,500	460,000
adio	50	63,500	33,005	7,875	7,700	575,000
lack and white TV	100	328,500	44,060	52,929	89,100	988,800
olor TV	435	1,180,000	158,013	215,350	27,000	5,884,900

port a radio and some form of television. The only variations evident are the relative number and type of television sets. The prices assigned to each type of item are presented in table 4.26. The overall figure for the household was obtained by simply adding the values, weighted by the actual number of individual items, to yield a total value of all communications equipment employed by the household (table 4.26).

Here, perhaps more than in any other functional area, the issue of whether more—as in more color televisions—is necessarily better appears to emerge. However, the reader must guard against falling into such evaluations. The domestic assets measure is designed to determine the condition of a household in terms of the physical equipment utilized to carry out specific household functions. The resulting measure is an economic evaluation of that equipment. It is also important to remember that disasters destroy this equipment, and households seek to replace these items when they are destroyed. Evaluations such as more is better will depend on one's definition of better, and they will not necessarily be reflected in the actual figure derived using our procedure.

Computing the Domestic Assets Scale

The final step in constructing the domestic assets measure is simply to add together the values of the domestic assets items employed in each of the ten functional areas, forming a composite index. Presented in table 4.27 are the descriptive statistics for each sample's domestic assets score. In addition, for limited comparisons, both the sample-specific and exchange dollar figures are presented. For presentation purposes, we have rank-ordered samples by the median dollar domestic assets figure. The ordering is probably very close to what one might have anticipated before seeing these figures, although the Turkish and

**Table 4.27. Descriptive Statistics
for Domestic Assets Scale**

Location	National Currency	Exchange ($)
United States		
Mean	71,560	71,560
Median	62,379	62,379
Italy		
Mean	78,262,396	40,667
Median	70,162,825	36,278
Yugoslavia		
Mean	8,208,993	27,922
Median	7,165,719	24,373
Mexico		
Mean	7,820,464	16,293
Median	5,408,937	11,269
Turkey		
Mean	6,529,126	11,180
Median	5,098,163	8,730
Peru		
Mean	134,001,615	11,652
Median	87,164,200	7,579

Peruvian figures are comparable, especially when the mean values are viewed. At this point, however, we would like to reserve discussion of the resulting index and these descriptive statistics until a satisfactory method of converting national currencies into international dollar figures has been introduced (table 4.27).

Chapter 5

Establishing a Common Monetary Unit Among Samples

In earlier chapters, problems associated with the Belcher cross-cultural level of living scale were discussed. One major problem concerned the weighting of items within functional areas and the subsequent weighting of functional areas relative to one another in creating the total score. The solution proposed by the domestic assets approach is to weight items by their cost in local markets. This solution overcomes the questionable and value-laden weighting of items according to their technological efficiency, and the total scale becomes self-weighting in that items requiring high capital expenditures are weighted more heavily in the total scale. While this solution overcomes many of the limitations of level of living scales, it introduces a problem when one is engaged in international research demanding cross-national comparisons. The problem, of course, is how domestic assets scores, calculated in the monetary units of different nations, should be converted into comparable monetary units to facilitate cross-national comparisons. This issue also rises for personnel in nongovernmental and governmental agencies wanting to employ the domestic assets measure to assess the effectiveness of programs in different countries.

Exchange and Purchasing Power Parity Conversions

Many solutions can be adopted when faced with this situation. Perhaps the simplest is to convert different currencies into a base currency—dollars, for example—by using prevailing international exchange rates at the time that data are collected. If data collection takes place over an extended period, or exchange rates fluctuate dramatically, one might simply compute an average exchange rate for the particular period of concern, or use average yearly exchange rates, or even use average exchange rates over several years. The latter solution is often adopted when cross-national data such as yearly GNP figures are compared.

While international exchange rates offer a straightforward solution, they also have a number of limitations. It is widely known that international exchange rates do not necessarily reflect true differences in the actual purchasing power of international currencies (Balassa 1964; Kravis, Heston, and Summers 1978a, 1978b, and 1982; Summers, Kravis, and Heston 1980). These rates are affected by many non-economic factors such as political situations and decisions. What is particularly limiting is the fact that international exchange rates are so responsive to international trade and monetary markets. These markets tend to be dominated and controlled by the world economy's most highly industrialized nations. As a result, the currencies of highly industrialized countries tend to be overvalued and those of less industrialized nations undervalued in exchange rates. The result of these unequal valuations is that comparisons based on exchange rates tend to favor industrialized nations, making their living conditions look even higher, and overestimate the extent of inequality between nations (Balassa 1964; Peacock, Hoover, and Killian, 1988). As a result, utilizing exchange rates to convert domestic assets scores that are designed to reflect differences in actual living conditions of households may bias and bring into question cross-national comparisons.

The problems inherent in exchange rates spawned a major United Nations project, termed the International Comparison Project, or ICP, that was designed to provide an alternative method of international comparisons (Kravis, Heston, and Summers 1978a, 1978b, 1982; Summers, Kravis, and Heston 1980; Summers and Heston 1984, 1988). As its objective, the ICP has to create currency conversions that allow for cross-national comparisons of aggregate income and production figures based on the purchasing power parity of world currencies. The hope is that these conversions will allow for more accurate comparisons of real incomes and production figures, not those based on a nation's power in the world economy or on political decisions.

In theory, the guiding principle behind this conversion is that international price comparisons should be based on the ratio of one country's prices to another country's prices for a common set of commodities and services. In practice, however, the picture is complicated by a number of difficulties. First, many commodities are not shared across nations. Some nations specialize in producing certain commodities, while others do not. In addition, the proportion of total national spending in particular areas, such as food, clothing, transportation, or construction, can vary across countries. This heterogeneous spending will alter the relative mix of purchasing power parities both across and within nations over time. Despite these problems and others, such as limited project resources and data availability, the ICP has been able to produce national income and production figures that facilitate spatial and temporal cross-national research of aggregate national statistics from 1950 to 1988 (Summers and Heston 1988).

For our purposes, a modified version of purchasing power parity conversions based on the logic employed by the ICP was utilized. It must be recalled that this study deals directly with comparing the concrete living conditions of households in specific sampling communities as assessed by the physical capital used by the household to carry out a specific set of domestic functions. As a result, we are not concerned with the great variety of goods and services that can be purchased by households or governments, nor are we concerned with the cost of capital goods or services utilized in production. Since we are dealing with a narrowly defined set of goods, and there is a high degree of comparability in this set of goods across countries, it seems reasonable to treat these goods as our common market basket. This basket will be utilized to compute a conversion ratio based on the relative purchasing power of each currency (using dollar figures as the base for comparison).

Specifically, the purchasing power parity conversion ($PPPCR_i$) utilized in this research will be derived from the following formula:

$$PPPCR_i = (\Sigma(P_{ij} / P_{usj}))/ N$$

Where $PPPCR_i$ is the conversion value utilized to convert country i's currency into international dollars, P_{ij} is the price of domestic asset j in country i, P_{usj} is the price of domestic asset j in the United States, and N is the total number of j domestic assets items that country i shares with the U.S. sample. Thus, the conversion factor is simply the average of the comparison ratios for a set of N domestic assets items shared between the countries of interest. It is possible that our conversion factor should be weighted to reflect proportion of income or investment in certain consumption areas. For example, if in a certain country a greater proportion of investment is in equipment used in food preparation, then these items could be weighted more heavily. Since such information was not readily available, however, it was decided to simply use the above version.

The critical assumption in this conversion is that we are indeed dealing with common sets of domestic assets items. As discussed in previous chapters, prices for domestic assets items were obtained by sampling retail establishments in each community. The actual items priced were highly detailed categories of capital goods used by households to carry out domestic functions. A list of items for which any price was obtained in the respective communities is presented in table A.1 of appendix A. The list shows that the highly detailed categories of items should have resulted in little intra-item heterogeneity. In addition, the pricing instrument included descriptions of each item in an attempt to insure that similar items were priced in each sample community. Because of the critical assumption of item comparability, it must be noted that construction costs have not been included in this analysis. Since these costs were based on construction quality categories that were allowed to vary across samples, comparability cannot be assumed. As a result, by including such items we would unnecessarily bias the analysis.

Taken as a whole, 90 domestic items had their prices recorded. Ideally, one would like to have prices for all 90 items across all sample sites. Unfortunately, this was not possible. A major reason for this lack was our simple inability to locate comparable items in all sample sites. The net result was that only 15 items were held in common across all sample communities. However, this is an inordinately restrictive ideal and, all things considered, would probably insure that only the most capital-intensive goods would be used for the conversion, which in turn would bias the conversion in favor of the U.S. sample. Therefore, it was decided that the common set of items would be allowed to vary across countries, utilizing the U.S. sample site as the base. This would permit us to maximize confidence in the conversion score obtained for any single country. Using this criterion, there were between 32 (Peruvian and U.S.) and 41 (Italian and U.S.) items held in common between each sample community and the U.S. sample.

In addition to procedural checks for item comparability, empirical tests for noncomparability of data were also undertaken. It can be assumed that between any two countries, items will be comparably priced in terms of their relative placement among all items. In other words, high-expense items in one country will be highly priced in another country relative to other items for sale. If this assumption is true, there should be a general linear relationship between the price of items between any two countries, and the extent to which an item deviates significantly from this trend should be an indicator of noncomparability. Thus, linear regression and subsequent diagnostic tests, exploring for outliers and influentials, were employed to empirically verify correspondence in items between the U.S. sample and each of the other sample sites. This analysis resulted in only two items being dropped from the original set. First, the prices associated with a component stereo system were dropped because there was clear deviation across all samples when compared to the U.S. sample data. Second, the formal dining table was significantly deviant for the Peruvian and Yugoslav samples when compared to the U.S. sample. As a result, these prices were dropped.

On the whole, the remaining items were highly comparable among all samples. The degree of linearity in prices between sample communities can be

Table 5.1. Correlations Between Prices of Domestic Assets Items Among Sample Communities

	United States	Italy	Yugoslavia	Mexico	Turkey
Italy	0.818				
	(41)				
Yugoslavia	0.559	0.420			
	(38)	(32)			
Mexico	0.739	0.668	0.711		
	(37)	(34)	(32)		
Turkey	0.784	0.610	0.635	0.780	
	(34)	(29)	(28)	(30)	
Peru	0.870	0.825	0.688	0.688	0.684
	(32)	(25)	(24)	(23)	(20)

Note: Figures in parentheses are base *N*s for the numbers directly above.

clearly seen in table 5.1, which presents the zero-order correlations between prices of similar items among the sample communities. All correlations are significant and reflect the anticipated strong-to-moderate positive relationship. The actual list of items that were utilized to create the purchasing power parity conversion for this research is presented in table A.2 in appendix A. To facilitate examination, all items have been deleted for which there was no price in the United States and in some other nation.

The next step in creating PPP conversion rates is the computation of ratios for each item. Presented in table A.3 of appendix A, these ratios represent the purchasing power, relative to a single U.S. dollar, of each country's currency when compared utilizing similar items. For example, examining purchasing power of currencies when a large refrigerator (item 4) is bought within our sample communities, we can see that one dollar is equal to 1,210 Italian lira, 242 Mexican pesos, 437 Yugoslav dinars, 12,984 Peruvian soles, and 361 Turkish lira. From even a cursory examination, one can also see that there are considerable variations in the conversion ratios within each sample. These variations reflect the actual variations in the purchasing power of currencies relative to the dollar for particular items.

Table 5.2 presents the descriptive statistics for each sample's conversion ratios. Examination of the minimum and maximum ratios for each country clearly shows the variation in the purchasing power of each currency across

Table 5.2. Descriptive Statistics of Conversion Ratios

	Italy	*Yugoslavia*	*Mexico*	*Turkey*	*Peru*
Mean	1,696.866	271.748	290.996	432.609	12,324.230
Median	1,560.000	212.628	240.823	330.621	12,565.106
SD	824.834	194.809	205.229	346.219	7,846.621
Minimum	425.581	43.153	43.939	33.898	2,444.737
Maximum	3,673.469	660.100	890.737	1,733.333	29,866.667
Range	3,247.888	616.947	846.798	1,699.435	27,421.930
N	41	38	37	34	32
Exchange rate	1,934.00	294.00	480.00	584.00	11,500.00
Exchange/PPP	1.14	1.08	1.65	1.35	0.93

domestic assets items. The conversion ratio to be used will be the average of the ratios, found in the first row of table 5.2. As anticipated, for four of the five sample sites, the PPP conversion ratio is lower than the international exchange rates, which are listed in the second to last row of this table. For example, if the ratio of exchange to purchasing power parity conversions is computed (see the table's last row), one can clearly see that in four of five sample communities the exchange rate tends to undervalue the local currency. The exception is the Peruvian sample. However, during the months of data collection the actual exchange rate changed dramatically, starting at 9,217 soles and ending at 12,835. Thus, the exchange rate presented is the average for that period. If we had utilized the final month's figures, the same pattern would have emerged. Considering that pricing probably reflects expected alterations in exchange rates because of expected inflation, the purchasing power parity conversion is not necessarily out of line with our general expectations.

In general, then, the above procedure, based on the same logic employed by the International Comparison Project, has produced a conversion method that should facilitate intersample comparisons of domestic assets scores. The conversion figures, and purchasing power parity dollars, produced by this method should facilitate comparisons because the conversion ratio is based on the actual purchasing power of each sample-specific currency relative to the U.S. sample for a common set of domestic assets items. In subsequent comparisons among samples, both the exchange and purchasing power parity conversions will be presented and utilized.

Chapter 6

The Validity and Reliability
of the Domestic Assets Measure

In chapter 4 we examined the Domestic Assets Scale's components, and in chapter 5 we discussed a method for converting domestic assets scores into international dollars that overcomes the potential problems associated with conversions based on exchange rates. This chapter will assess the Domestic Assets Scale's reliability and validity.

Before such an examination, however, it is important to address the unique nature of this study and its implications for reliability and validity assessment. It will be recalled that this research was conducted in six communities located in different countries. These studies can be thought of as six independent replications of research designed to develop and assess the utility of the domestic assets measure. Given the study's design, reliability and validity analysis will be undertaken in a twofold manner. First, validity and reliability will be assessed within each sample as if each represented an independent replication of the same study. At this stage of the analysis, the findings both within and among the samples will be critical factors in assessing the measure's validity and reliability. If the measure performs in a consistently positive manner across all samples, confidence in the measure will be greatly enhanced.

The second stage of this analysis will consist of an evaluation of all the data combined into a single data set. While each of these samples can be thought of as an independent replication, the samples themselves were selected to reflect a range of cultural areas and levels of economic development. If we turn to economic development, the samples were selected to reflect a range of nations including high incomes (U.S. and Italy), moderate incomes (Yugoslavia and Mexico), and low incomes (Turkey and Peru). Using World Bank classifications, the latter two countries would actually be classified as lower middle income. Unfortunately, because of budget constraints, we were unable to include very-low-income countries in this project. Nevertheless, the countries included can be treated as examples of different types of nations, and combining their results will allow for evaluating the domestic assets measure across a fuller range of living conditions than would be present within a single country. Therefore, the reliability and validity of this measure will also be assessed using all observations combined into a single overall sample.

To combine the independent samples into a single data set, the domestic assets scores and other monetary units were converted to a common metric—international dollars—using both exchange rates and the modified purchasing power parity conversion developed in chapter 5. The exchange rates employed were based on prevailing rates at the time of data collection. The PPP conversion is the average ratio between the cost of each particular domestic asset item (i.e., particular types of refrigerators, stoves, sinks, etc.) in the respective sample community and the equivalent item's cost in the U.S. sample. Overall, we would expect the PPP conversion to reflect the actual value of a given living condition in each community, when compared to the living conditions in the U.S. sample community, better than exchange rate comparisons.

In the process of combining the individual samples into a single overall data set, it is possible to entertain the idea of differentially weighting each sample to be representative of the world system of societies. Unfortunately, as mentioned above, our samples do not reflect the full range of societies since very poor nations have not been included and there are no samples from African or Asian societies. Therefore, no attempt is being made to utilize these data to represent all nations in the world system. However, it does not seem reasonable simply to combine these samples, which themselves are different in size. Instead, the samples were differentially weighted so that each represents one-sixth of the combined data set. This will insure that samples with higher Ns do not overly influence the results.

Reliability Analysis

Implied by the concept of reliability is the notion of consistency in measurement, especially as it relates to a measure's internal components (Carmines and Zeller 1979). In other words, a measure's internal components are expected to behave in a consistently similar manner for the measure itself to be considered reliable. The Domestic Assets Scale is proposed as a measure of a household's physical living conditions. However, it would be unreasonable to suggest that this measure assesses a single dimension. As a measure of overall household living conditions, the scale seeks to capture the various dimensions of these conditions by assessing ten functional areas. In the accumulation process, households would not be expected to simultaneously raise living conditions across each of these areas. It is likely that accumulation is concentrated in specific areas first, while other areas lag behind until sufficient capital is available to purchase equipment. The specific areas in which expenditures occur first will be a function of culture, community infrastructure, and level of national development, among other factors.

Nevertheless, despite the fact that accumulation will not equally occur across all functional areas, it can be expected that a general positive correlation should exist between all functional areas. Furthermore, a degree of consistency should be present. As a result, following standard approaches, this measure's reliability is assessed in terms of its internal consistency across functional areas (Carmines and Zeller 1979; Zeller and Carmines 1980); specifically, internal consistency is assessed by examining the inter-item correlations among the monetary values of items used in each area. The first step in this assessment is an examination of the separate samples.

The inter-item correlations among the ten functional areas for each sample community are presented in table 6.1, which has been broken down into six panels. Examination of these results indicates that the expectation of positive correlations among the ten functional areas holds and that this pattern is consistent across sample communities. Indeed, all of the statistically significant correlations presented indicate positive correlations. Some variations exist in the magnitudes of these correlations and in the number of correlations that are significant. One hundred percent of the 45 possible correlations are significant and positive in the Mexican and Peruvian samples, 96 percent in the U.S. and Turkish samples, 93 percent in the Yugoslav, and 64 percent in the Italian. The Italian sample yields the fewest significant correlations. Further examination of this matrix indicates that the items for clothes washing and water heating are particularly problematic. If these functional areas are dropped from the analysis, 86 percent of the remaining possible correlations are significant.

The problems with these two items in the Italian data are potentially a result of insufficient specificity on the questionnaire that resulted in an attenuation of the variance for these items. Examination of the data on clothes washing equipment (not presented here) indicates that more than 92.2 percent of the households were coded as having an automatic washing machine, which resulted in little variation. Perhaps this item should be refined to capture greater variation among automatic washers. The problems with the water heating items stem from both the interview instrument and the price survey. While sufficient variability was recorded during the household interviews, pricing information resulted in more than 80 percent of the households being assigned the same value. In addition, nonautomatic water heaters were assigned higher values

Table 6.1. Inter-Item Correlations Among the Ten Functional Areas for Each Sample Community

Functional Areas	(1)	(2)	(3)	(4)	(5)	(6)	(7)	(8)	(9)
United States (N=233)									
1. Shelter	—								
2. Food preservation	.5911*	—							
3. Food preparation	.5100*	.6351*	—						
4. Clothes washing	.5980*	.5164*	.4514*	—					
5. Dishwashing	.4780*	.4311*	.5561*	.4681*	—				
6. Bathing	.8009*	.5918*	.4754*	.6127*	.4919*	—			
7. Waste disposal	.7558*	.5407*	.4366*	.5649*	.5447*	.8027*	—		
8. Sleeping	.6260*	.4434*	.3314*	.3205*	.3247*	.6051*	.6118*	—	
9. Water heating	.2672*	.2191*	.2236*	.1882*	.0838	.2704*	.1543*	.0806	—
10. Communication	.7972*	.5964*	.5217*	.4744*	.3625*	.7247*	.7077*	.6277*	.2782*
Italy (N=214)									
1. Shelter	—								
2. Food preservation	.0777	—							
3. Food preparation	.1655*	.1957*	—						
4. Clothes washing	.0916†	.0883†	.1150#	—					
5. Dishwashing	.3049*	.1340#	.0805	.1660*	—				
6. Bathing	.5719*	.1553*	.0982†	.0571	.2923*	—			
7. Waste disposal	.4717*	.1658*	.1208#	.0893†	.2936*	.8438*	—		
8. Sleeping	.2207*	.1217#	.2176*	.1044†	.0441	.2007*	.2897*	—	
9. Water heating	.0457	.1629*	-.0427	.0412	.1184#	.1002†	.0383	-.0734	—
10. Communication	.2748*	.1815*	.1582*	-.0225	.2175*	.2656*	.2636*	.2193*	.1306*

Yugoslavia (N=279)

	1	2	3	4	5	6	7	8	9
1. Shelter	—								
2. Food preservation	.4031*	—							
3. Food preparation	.1497*	.2791*	—						
4. Clothes washing	.1967*	.2611*	.2432*	—					
5. Dishwashing	.1593*	.2553*	.1804*	.1358*	—				
6. Bathing	.2744*	.2726*	.1338*	.4704*	.1621*	—			
7. Waste disposal	.3564*	.2332*	.1538*	.1877*	.1328*	.3568*	—		
8. Sleeping	.2859*	.1499*	.1714*	.1423*	.1202#	.2333*	.2103*	—	
9. Water heating	.1046#	.1544*	.0785†	.3363*	.0515	.3694*	.2893*	.0329	—
10. Communication	.2549*	.3633*	.3032*	.3350*	.2828*	.3121*	.2098*	.1435*	.2461*

Mexico (N=312)

	1	2	3	4	5	6	7	8	9
1. Shelter	—								
2. Food preservation	.3947*	—							
3. Food preparation	.2770*	.4002*	—						
4. Clothes washing	.2833*	.4289*	.2195*	—					
5. Dishwashing	.2001*	.2107*	.1209#	.2003*	—				
6. Bathing	.5759*	.5885*	.3153*	.5202*	.2947*	—			
7. Waste disposal	.5531*	.5428*	.3225*	.4738*	.2474*	.8404*	—		
8. Sleeping	.4370*	.4714*	.3397*	.2657*	.2251*	.4609*	.4776*	—	
9. Water heating	.3630*	.3703*	.2777*	.3979*	.2460*	.6413*	.4684*	.2535*	—
10. Communication	.3246*	.4338*	.2614*	.5068*	.1975*	.5463*	.5166*	.3178*	.4362*

Turkey (N=315)

	1	2
1. Shelter	—	
2. Food preservation	.2078*	—

Table 6.1 (*Continued*)

Functional Areas	(1)	(2)	(3)	(4)	(5)	(6)	(7)	(8)	(9)
3. Food preparation	.1800*	.1269*							
4. Clothes washing	.2888*	.2279*	.3407*						
5. Dishwashing	.1867*	.1497*	.1595*	.2616*					
6. Bathing	.1942*	.2719*	.2593*	.3225*	.3919*				
7. Waste disposal	.4458*	.3156#	.2691*	.3853*	.3226*	.4194*			
8. Sleeping	.1621*	.1053#	.1267*	.0914#	.0206	−.0312	.1937*		
9. Water heating	.2569*	.1547*	.2765*	.4476*	.3857*	.4230*	.2853*	.1483*	
10. Communication	.4181*	.2953*	.2537*	.3933*	.2861*	.3260*	.3382*	.1138#	.3342*
Peru (N=309)									
1. Shelter	—								
2. Food preservation	.2919*	—							
3. Food preparation	.2252*	.2991*	—						
4. Clothes washing	.2345*	.1541*	.3193*	—					
5. Dishwashing	.2853*	.3279*	.3598*	.2755*	—				
6. Bathing	.4720*	.3268*	.3937*	.2689*	.3530*	—			
7. Waste disposal	.5156*	.3314*	.4932*	.4584*	.4825*	.7094*	—		
8. Sleeping	.3598*	.2368*	.2612*	.3158*	.2488*	.3627*	.4250*	—	
9. Water heating	.3024*	.2362*	.4362*	.2833*	.4330*	.3998*	.4972*	.2125*	—
10. Communication	.2836*	.3359*	.5422*	.3651*	.4248*	.4241*	.5654*	.3373*	.4741*

* = prob(r) ≤ .01; † = prob(r) ≤ .10; # = prob(r) ≤ .05.

than automatic and central boiler systems. This pattern occurred in no other sample community. It appears that greater specificity with respect to the initial coding and subsequent pricing could have resulted in greater variance and more significant correlations among these items. Thus, the potential problems in the Italian data are not a function of a flawed measure, but point to needed improvements in the collection procedure.

Despite variations in the magnitude of the correlations within each sample, the overall pattern is consistent with the expected positive correlations. Indeed, all of the statistically significant correlations are positive. Computing average correlations for each sample, including all correlations, indicates that there are again variations across samples; nevertheless, the expectations hold. The average correlations were highest in the U.S. data (.482), followed by the Mexican (.383), Peruvian (.363), Turkish (.256), Yugoslav (.226), and Italian (.174). The internal consistency can further be assessed by using a conventional measure of inter-item reliability such as Cronbach's alpha (1951). The highest alpha was computed for the U.S. sample (.903), followed by the Mexican (.861), Peruvian (.851), Turkish (.775), Yugoslav (.745), and Italian (.680). These alphas are of sufficient magnitude to suggest a pattern of internal consistency within each sample, and this pattern holds across all sample communities. Thus, while there is clearly room for improvement, especially in the Italian case, the results suggest the measure's high degree of reliability when the overall pattern across sample communities is considered.

Combining the results into a single data set will allow for an assessment of the domestic assets measure's reliability considering a greater range of possible living conditions. Inter-item correlations across all functional areas are presented in table 6.2. This table has been divided into two panels, with the first panel displaying the inter-item correlations for the data converted into a common metric using the PPP conversions, and the second panel presenting the data based on exchange dollar conversions. Examination shows that all 45 correlations are significant and positive, as expected. On the whole, these correlations are generally higher than those of any one of the independent samples. In part, this results from the fact that the combined data set includes a fuller range of physical living conditions. Indeed, the average correlation for the upper panel is .469, and for the lower panel it is .549. Computing Cronbach's alpha for each panel yields the very high values of .898 for the upper and .924 for the lower panel. These results again suggest a high degree of reliability, as assessed by internal consistency.

Considering both stages of the above analysis, we can conclude that the Domestic Assets Scale is indeed a reliable measure. While there was some

Table 6.2. Inter-Item Correlations Among the Ten Functional Areas for the Combined Data Set

Functional Areas	(1)	(2)	(3)	(4)	(5)	(6)	(7)	(8)	(9)
Price conversions based on purchasing power parity conversions									
1. Shelter	—								
2. Food preservation	.4575*	—							
3. Food preparation	.6210*	.6351*	—						
4. Clothes washing	.5784*	.3737*	.5138*	—					
5. Dishwashing	.5428*	.3105*	.6754*	.4629*	—				
6. Bathing	.4636*	.4182*	.2506*	.2703*	.0609*	—			
7. Waste disposal	.6309*	.4572*	.5049*	.3396*	.3401*	.7465*	—		
8. Sleeping	.6353*	.2225*	.5390*	.5001*	.5649*	.1426*	.3433*	—	
9. Water heating	.5083*	.4269*	.5906*	.4739*	.6383*	.2188*	.3739*	.4637*	—
10. Communication	.7081*	.4954*	.6096*	.5594*	.4997*	.4280*	.5465*	.5738*	.5332*
Price conversions based on exchange rates									
1. Shelter	—								
2. Food preservation	.5236*	—							
3. Food preparation	.6829*	.5533*	—						
4. Clothes washing	.6289*	.4235*	.5608*	—					
5. Dishwashing	.6429*	.3883*	.7379*	.5166*	—				
6. Bathing	.5197*	.5260*	.3625*	.3738*	.2040*	—			
7. Waste disposal	.7114*	.5680*	.6287*	.4602*	.5370*	.7120*	—		
8. Sleeping	.6971*	.3984*	.6132*	.5417*	.6435*	.2329*	.4728*	—	
9. Water heating	.5968*	.4849*	.6499*	.5029*	.6783*	.3375*	.5497*	.5395*	—
10. Communication	.7691*	.5581*	.6812*	.5994*	.5864*	.4977*	.6449*	.6467*	.6037*

* = prob(r) ≤ .01.

variation across samples when they were considered independently, the results indicate high to moderate degrees of internal consistency, and these results are consistent across all samples. The results of the combined sample suggest a highly reliable measure.

Validity Analysis

A construct validation will be undertaken to assess the overall validity of the domestic assets measure (Cronbach and Meehl 1955; Carmines and Zeller 1979; Zeller and Carmines 1980). In establishing validity, it was reasoned that the Domestic Assets Scale as a measure of household physical living conditions should be related to (1) the level of economic development of the country in which the sample community resides, (2) measures associated with the household's ability to accumulate and maintain a set of living conditions, and (3) other measures associated with a household's socioeconomic status, or level of living. The overall validity of this measure will be assessed with respect to the above assumptions and will be examined within and across samples, with consistency being imperative. It will also be examined using the combined sample.

The first step consists of comparing sample results to the levels of development across nations. The communities in which our random samples were drawn were selected to be roughly similar with respect to their niche in each country's political economy. All sample communities are medium-size cities compared to the distribution of city sizes within each country. They are provincial cities rather than major administrative centers, and only light industries are incorporated into their social structures. No claim is made that they represent the economy of the whole country, and the figures to be presented should not be generalized beyond the particular units studied. However, the degree to which the sample communities are similar should allow for rough comparisons across samples. It is anticipated that mean and median domestic assets scores for each community should replicate the ordering of nations based on GNP per capita. As discussed above, the nations were selected to reflect a range of societies in terms of development and culture. With respect to development, the samples fall into three broad categories, high-income nations (U.S. and Italian samples), high-middle-income countries (Yugoslavia and Mexico), and lower-middle-income countries (Turkey and Peru). Indeed, the samples can be rank-ordered, using GNP per capita, in the following sequence: U.S., Italian, Yugoslav, Mexican, Turkish, and Peruvian. If the Domestic Assets Scale is measuring the relative cost of establishing a set of living conditions, and if it can be assumed that sample selection will allow rough comparisons across sites, then the typical household's domestic assets, in terms of the mean and median, should follow this same order.

Table 6.3 presents the mean and median domestic assets values in national currencies, exchange dollars, and purchasing power parity dollars for each sample community. The communities have been arranged in decreasing order, with high-income countries listed first, followed by lower-income nations. Examination of the means and medians for both exchange and PPP conversion figures replicates the rank-ordering anticipated. The only exception is the mean figure for exchange dollars in Peru, which is slightly higher than the Turkish sample's mean figure. However, in light of the skewed nature of assets in each sample community, it would be preferable to use the median as the measure of central tendency. Employing the median figure results in a pattern consistent with our expectations.

The next step in assessing the measure's validity was to examine the correlations between it and other measures. Specifically, since the domestic assets measure was designed to assess overall household living conditions, it should be related to factors that affect domestic assets accumulation as well as factors normally associated with the quality of living conditions. These factors can be classified into three categories. The first consists of three factors related to household economic attainment and maintenance of living conditions: total household income, education of male head of household, and age of male head of household. Each of these can be thought of as determinants of a household's living conditions, and these factors should be positively associated with the value of domestic assets.

The second set of items consists of a number of factors that should be positively correlated with domestic assets because they too are roughly associated with the overall economic cost of establishing a set of living conditions. The first is the amount of money paid by the household for rent, if the dwelling unit is rented. It will be assumed that higher rent is required for higher-quality dwelling units, and, as a result, the amount paid should be positively related to domestic assets. Also included are three measures related to the size of the actual living area, average room size, square meters per person, and rooms per person. The expectation is that each of these items should be positively associated with domestic assets.

Two additional items are included in this set. The first is a simple additive level of living measure that was created by scoring a household based on its having or not having 20 items usually associated with level of living scales such as electricity, refrigerators, flush toilets, and running water. A house-

Table 6.3. Descriptive Statistics for Domestic Assets Scale

Location	National Currency	Exchange ($)	PPP ($)
United States			
Mean	71,560	71,560	71,560
Median	62,379	62,379	62,379
Italy			
Mean	78,262,396	40,467	46,122
Median	70,162,825	36,278	41,348
Yugoslavia			
Mean	8,208,993	27,922	30,208
Median	7,165,719	24,373	26,368
Mexico			
Mean	7,820,464	16,293	26,875
Median	5,408,937	11,269	18,588
Turkey			
Mean	6,574,332	11,257	15,197
Median	5,117,975	8,764	11,830
Peru			
Mean	134,001,615	11,652	10,830
Median	87,164,200	7,579	7,072

hold received a score of 1 for each of the 20 items they possessed. It was expected that there should be a positive correlation between the additive level of living measure and the Domestic Assets Scale. The final validity item was a simple dichotomous variable indicating whether the household owned an automobile. There should be a positive correlation between domestic assets and the possession of an automobile, although it should be relatively stronger in less-developed than in high-income nations. The logic behind this statement is that, in high-income nations, transportation is considered a necessity and financial credit is structured so that larger proportions of households can acquire automobiles.

The final items are indicators of household expenditure patterns. Specifically, these items assess the household's average monthly spending on electricity; transportation, whether public or private; clothing; food; and total average monthly expenditures on food, clothing, transportation, and energy.

The correlations between the domestic assets measure and the validity measures are in table 6.4, which presents the correlations for each sample commu-

Table 6.4. Correlations Between Domestic Assets Scale and Validity Measures

	Independent Sample Communities						Combined Sample	
	United States	*Italy*	*Yugoslavia*	*Mexico*	*Turkey*	*Peru*	*PPP*	*Exchange*
Attainment items								
(1)	.6887*	.4595*	.5355*	.2345*	.3749*	.3873*	.7594*	.7927*
(2)	—	.3452*	.2044*	.3033*	.2801*	—	.2676*	.3009*
(3)	—	.0828	.1590*	.1921*	−.042	.2716*	.2149*	.2347*
Socioeconomic status items								
(4)	.7756*	.6817*	−.025	.3579*	.2998*	.7256*	.6144*	.6889*
(5)	.6619*	.4064*	.3410*	.5195*	.4798*	.4537*	.6740*	.6800*
(6)	.7196*	.6249*	.0957	.4642*	.4062*	.5098*	.1961*	.1539*
(7)	—	.1874*	.4802*	.3826*	.2111*	.5120*	.4063*	.4379*
(8)	—	.5221*	.5211*	.8035*	.4438*	.6898*	.5068*	.5209*
(9)	.0584	.1491*	.2512*	.3463*	.2891*	.3072*	.5099*	.5066*
Consumption items								
(10)	.7233*	.2655*	.3151*	.3343*	.4050*	.1747*	.7441*	.7792*
(11)	.5375*	.0819	.2204*	.3982*	.2822*	.2509*	.6261*	.6627*
(12)	.6569*	.3732*	.2813*	.4485*	.3077*	.2329*	.7489*	.7809*
(13)	.7077*	.2713*	.3305*	.3372*	.3616*	.0946*	.7569*	.7907*
Total	.7260*	.2818*	.3943*	.4306*	.4174*	.1731*	.7673*	.8163*

*Significant at the .01 level.

(1) Total household income
(2) Education of male head of household
(3) Age of male head of household
(4) Amount of money paid by household for rent
(5) Level of living measure for household
(6) Average room size
(7) Rooms per person
(8) Square meters per person
(9) Household ownership of an automobile
(10) Household's average monthly spending on electricity
(11) Household's average monthly spending on transportation
(12) Household's average monthly spending on clothing
(13) Household's average monthly spending on food

nity considered separately and for the combined sample as well. The correlations between the Domestic Assets Scale and items indicating income, rents, or consumption for each of the sample communities are based on measures taken in local sample-specific currencies. The data used to calculate correlations for the combined sample were converted into international dollars using both exchange and purchasing power parity conversions. The latter correlations are presented in the table's final two columns.

Focusing first on the relationship between the Domestic Assets Scale and attainment items, it can clearly be seen that the expected pattern prevails. Income is positively associated with the assets measure. It is interesting to note that the correlations are relatively stronger in high-income than in low-income nations. A traditional problem for researchers in low-income countries is that income is difficult to measure because of the lack of salary and wage labor and the relative importance of subsistence or use value production (Ramsey and Collazo 1960; Ugalde 1970). In addition, income is not always a good measure of actual household socioeconomic status and level of living. These correlations are consistent with previous research findings and strongly suggest the strength of the Domestic Assets Scale as an overall measure of household physical living conditions. The correlations with income for the combined sample are very strong and positive. Similar patterns emerge when the correlations for education and age of head of household are examined. However, the correlations for age in the Italian and Turkish samples are not significant. Nevertheless, those for the combined sample are both positive and significant. Overall, the expectations of positive significant correlations between domestic assets and attainment items hold.

The correlations between the Domestic Assets Scale and other items often associated with socioeconomic status are presented in the middle section of table 6.4. The vast majority of these correlations are consistent with our expectations of positive significance. In general, rent, level of living, average room size, rooms per person, square meters per person, and having at least one automobile are all positively correlated with the domestic assets measure, both within sample-specific and combined sample results. The only exceptions occur in the Yugoslav and U.S. samples. In the Yugoslav sample, rents and average room size are not correlated with the domestic assets measure. However, this result might have been expected, given the Yugoslav government's ideological commitment to egalitarianism as well as extensive governmental control of housing and rents. While simple possession of an automobile is not correlated in the U.S. sample, additional analysis (not presented here) indicates that the number and value of automobiles are correlated. Thus, for the United

States, a nation that has become highly dependent on private transportation, it is the number and value of automobiles—rather than the possession of one—that are related to domestic assets. The overall consistency of these results, both within each independent sample and as a combined data set, further suggests the validity of the Domestic Assets Scale.

The final correlations to be considered are those between the Domestic Assets Scale and consumption or expenditure data for each household. These correlations are presented in the lower section of table 6.4. While there is some variability in the magnitudes of these correlations across sample communities, all except one are significant and positive, as expected. Indeed, examination of the correlations for the combined data set yields very strong correlations between household expenditures and domestic assets.

Conclusions

Taken as a whole, the results from the validity and reliability analysis strongly suggest that the Domestic Assets Scale is a reliable and valid measure of household physical living conditions. In regard to this statement, it must be remembered that we are not claiming that the measure captures all facets of household living conditions. However, if one is attempting to assess living conditions in terms of the actual physical conditions under which a household lives and performs normal domestic functions, then the Domestic Assets Scale offers both a reliable and valid measure. In addition, the consistency of these results across independent samples and utilizing the combined data suggests that the domestic assets measure is valid and reliable for use in cross-cultural and cross-national research. Indeed, utilizing either exchange or purchasing power parity conversions offers researchers the ability to apply the same measures to a great variety of cultural and economic situations.

When used in disaster studies, the Domestic Assets Scale must be employed in connection with a damage and loss assessment technique. Interview schedules must include a set of questions that elicit information on the disaster's impact on each domestic asset. For example, after determining which type of equipment a household uses or used to cook its food, it is necessary to ask a question such as the following: What happened to your kitchen stove in the earthquake? After recording how the item was affected, it is necessary to rate the extent of damage on a scale such as the following: (1) destroyed or lost (100 percent loss); (2) badly damaged—cannot be used without extensive repairs (66 percent loss); (3) slightly damaged—can be used after minor repairs (33 percent loss); (4) undamaged—not damaged or so slightly damaged that it is still usable (0 percent loss). Using these percentages, the value assigned to the item can be reduced in much the same way as the value of a damaged item is depreciated for insurance purposes. By doing this with each domestic asset item, and then by accumulating item scores, a total depreciated domestic assets score can be calculated. This score measures the absolute loss in domestic assets for a household in a disaster. Because the original scale gives higher weight to more costly items, and because the damage score is based on this self-weighting method, it too is self-weighting. It also has the same cross-cultural qualities as the Domestic Assets Scale.

In longitudinal disaster studies, the domestic assets score can be employed to reconstruct a household's pre-disaster situation as well as to measure the re-accumulation of domestic assets following impact. To measure the pre-disaster situation, the interviewer asks such questions as: What did you cook your food on at the time of the earthquake? This is, of course, followed by the damage estimation questions. To assess recovery, the same household is reinterviewed at regular intervals into the reconstruction period—for example, every six months for three years. In each interview the domestic assets being employed at that time are recorded and given a monetary cost weight. Thus, if a household is on the path to recovery, the domestic assets score will increase toward the level found at the time just before the disaster. This same method was employed in the Guatemalan Earthquake Study and proved its value as a means of monitoring recovery (Bates 1982; Killian and Bates 1982; Killian, Peacock, and Bates 1982, 1983, 1984; Bates, Killian, and Peacock 1984; Peacock, Killian, Hoover, and Bates 1984; Peacock, Killian, and Bates 1987; Rodeheaver 1990). Since this version of the Domestic Assets Scale has been improved and tested on an international and cross-cultural basis, it should prove even more useful. The following chapter will discuss its further uses.

Chapter 7

Summary and Conclusions

The research on which this monograph is based rests on the premise that disaster researchers in the social sciences need a set of pretested, cross-culturally valid measuring instruments for use in evaluating the impact of disasters on human systems. This need stems not only from the normal requirement for measuring instruments in any type of research but, in the case of disasters, from the nature of the research problem itself.

Disasters are relatively rare events in any given geographical or cultural setting. Therefore, the accumulation of knowledge on disasters as social as well as physical processes requires the accumulation of knowledge by the comparison of cases occurring in many different sociocultural and geographic contexts. In addition, culture and social organization, as well as the affected community's level of social and economic development, are known to play significant roles in the disaster process, and we need to understand these roles through comparative cross-cultural research.

Furthermore, most disasters are sudden, more or less unexpected events whose physical impact occurs during a brief period. The social phenomena associated with disasters begin immediately, sometimes even before impact, and unfold rapidly. This means that disaster researchers must get into the field as quickly as possible, and, if they are to be effective, they must arrive with already pretested data collection plans and instruments. Even so, for most disaster research it is necessary, using retrospective methods, to reconstruct the pre-disaster situation of the social systems under study. Frequently it also is necessary to reconstruct early events in the emergency period.

For these reasons, this research is based on the premise that carefully pretested, cross-culturally valid instruments for measuring disaster impact, which are amenable to retrospective reconstruction, are needed in advance of most disaster studies. Such pretested instruments could form a readily available tool kit that disaster researchers could immediately take into the field.

A third characteristic of disasters that has significance for research methodology is the fact that they are unfolding events which occur as a process, sometimes extending over a decade or more. This means that longitudinal research designs are required to deal with the whole disaster process. Such a design requires instruments that can be used to measure the same variables repeatedly so that the entire disaster process can be accurately monitored. This research, therefore, has been aimed toward developing a measuring scale that can be used not only to assess disaster impact and to reconstruct the predisaster situation, but to measure the recovery or reconstruction process as it unfolds following impact.

The Nature of the Domestic Assets Scale

Many dimensions of the social impact of disasters require study. For example, disasters have emotional impacts on disaster victims. They produce deaths and physical injuries as well as health problems, and, by so doing, affect various social units such as families, medical facilities and personnel, and emergency workers and emergency organizations and groups. Disasters also have political ramifications and impacts on community governmental structures. They affect businesses and industries and have impacts on transportation, communications systems, public utilities such as water, and power systems. This list could go on almost endlessly, but it serves to illustrate that no single impact measure can serve all research needs. It further points to the need for developing a whole tool kit of pretested instruments ready for use in future disaster studies.

The research reported on in this book develops one such instrument whose purpose is limited to measuring the impact of physically destructive disasters on household living conditions. This instrument, the Domestic Assets Scale, is specifically designed to be cross-culturally valid and useful in any disaster that produces a serious physical impact on housing and household possessions. It is meant to serve as a criterion variable capable of measuring physical living conditions on a longitudinal basis. By combining it with a damage assessment method, it can be used to measure disaster losses in living conditions and therefore as a measure of impact. In addition, it can be used to measure changes in living conditions and can be employed as a measure of reconstruction and recovery at the household level. Because it can be employed in these ways, it can also be used to measure development at the household level if the researcher is willing to assume that changes in living conditions can serve as a measure of development.

Review of the Theoretical Basis of the Research

The Domestic Assets Scale is a modification of the Belcher Cross-Cultural
Level of Living Scale and of previous level of living scales (cf. Chapin 1938;
Sewell 1940, 1943; Hagood and Ducoff 1944; Sharp and Ramsey 1963; Belcher
1972). It has redesigned such scales to fit the needs of cross-cultural disaster
research and to improve the means of scoring such instruments so that this
scale has a sounder theoretical foundation. A rather simple, clear-cut theoretical underpinning was used as the basis for index construction. It can be stated
as follows:

1. In all societies, households, which consist of a group of people sharing a
common dwelling unit, establish a set of physical living conditions that supply
them with an artificially constructed environment on which they depend for the
performance of a set of household functions.

2. A set of common household functions can be identified that are performed
in households around the world. These functions center on such things as shelter; water supply; food storage, processing, and consumption; sanitation; and
communications.

3. To perform these functions, people in all societies employ items of physical technology that make up their physical living conditions. These items,
which are called domestic assets, include housing and household equipment
and facilities; together, they provide the artificial environment through which
the household sustains itself as a social unit by performing its functions.

4. To acquire these items of technology, the household must make a monetary investment. Each item of technology is associated with an acquisition cost,
and the cost of the total set of items represents the household's investment in
its living conditions.

5. What differs from one household to another in a given society or between
households in different societies is the type of technological item, or domestic
asset, employed to perform a given function. Poor households in societies with
less highly developed economic and technological systems employ relatively
primitive low-cost domestic assets, while rich households use costly, high-tech
items for the same purpose.

6. By assessing the economic value of the domestic assets constituting a
household's living conditions, a score can be arrived at which places that household on a scale relative to others (a) in their own society or community or (b) to
households in other societies or communities with respect to the economic
value of the domestic assets they employ. This score represents the total value
of the domestic assets associated with a household.

7. High physical impact disasters damage and destroy household living conditions. Different types of disasters affect various types of domestic assets differently and therefore produce different types and levels of loss for different households. These losses can be assessed by estimating the degree of damage to each asset and depreciating its value by that amount.

8. Because domestic assets are physical items, and because they are easily remembered by disaster victims and can be verified through on-site inspection by field-workers, it is possible to reconstruct the pre-disaster living conditions of a household with relative accuracy. This is important because both damage and loss must be assessed against this benchmark and because recovery also must be measured relative to it.

9. Because reconstruction involves the restoration of household living conditions, the Domestic Assets Scale can be used at successive periods during the process to measure relative recovery.

10. Finally, because disasters, and especially recovery, cannot be separated from social and economic development, it is important to be able to measure a household's level of development. Disasters are associated with a society's level of technological development since technology can prevent or cause disasters. It is also possible that disasters may produce positive or negative development. It is therefore important to be able to measure disaster impact in terms that lend themselves to relating disasters to development. The Domestic Assets Scale is especially useful because it can be used to monitor development by assuming that an increase in the level of domestic assets represents developmental change.

An Evaluation of the Domestic Assets Scale

In previous chapters an analysis of data collected to evaluate the Domestic Assets Scale has been presented. This analysis supports the following conclusions:

1. The various items included in the scale representing individual domestic assets items seem to be measuring the same variable when those items are represented by their replacement value. This means essentially that there is internal consistency among items so that poor households more or less consistently use low-cost domestic assets to perform household functions and rich households use high-cost items. This conclusion holds true for all six sample cities in six different countries varying in levels of economic development. In addition, the measure displays a remarkable degree of internal consistency when the samples were combined into a single data set, thereby allowing for an assessment of internal consistency over a fuller range of possible living conditions.

2. The domestic assets score for households, which represents the total cost of the collection of domestic assets items included in the scale, correlates relatively well with the set of other measures or variables used to establish its validity. These validation measures included income, education of the household head, age of the household head, as well as other variables thought of as measuring socioeconomic status. In other words, the Domestic Assets Scale, which measures the cost of establishing a set of household physical living conditions, correlates with other measures related to a household's economic standing. These relationships held within and across the six sample cities, showing that the Domestic Assets Scale works in about the same way in different cultural settings in societies that vary in levels of social and economic development. In addition, when utilizing the combined data, the measure displayed the expected pattern of correlation with other validity measures.

3. When the mean and median domestic assets scores for each of the six sample cities were ranked and compared to data on GNP per capita for the countries in which they were located, the ranks for GNP per capita and for domestic assets corresponded. This comparison required transforming scores for each country into dollars, using both exchange rates and the purchasing power parity method. The results demonstrate that the Domestic Assets Scale is capable of placing households in different countries with different levels of social and economic development on a single scale that correctly places sample communities relative to each other.

4. This particular project did not test a damage assessment method in the study communities because there was no disaster against which to test them. However, such a method was tested in the Guatemalan Earthquake Study and later was used with the items from this current study in interviews with households in Mexico City following the 1985 earthquake there. This method, which depreciates the value of each domestic asset according to the degree of damage, worked reasonably well under realistic fieldwork conditions where nonexpert, but trained, interviewers were employed.

On the basis of these results, the conclusion that the Domestic Assets Scale is a reliable and valid measure of disaster impact on household living conditions is warranted. There are, however, some problems associated with cross-cultural comparisons that require further comment.

Problems of Cross-Cultural Comparisons

The comparison of disaster impacts among events occurring in different cultural settings requires the use of scales or indices that measure the same variable in the same manner in all settings. The Domestic Assets Scale seeks cross-cultural applicability by use of the logic stated in the theoretical argument presented here. Basically, this argument rests on the assumption that (a) there is a common set of domestic functions that applies to all households in all cultural settings and (b) that everywhere these functions are performed by use of items of material culture that have an economic cost associated with them. The reasoning is that comparability can be achieved by examining the items of material culture used to perform a common set of functions and by evaluating their relative costs. This reasoning raises a set of issues concerning the possible bias brought in by these assumptions.

One issue concerns the possibility of a Western bias introduced by the Domestic Assets Scale's materialistic nature and by the fact that it uses economic value or replacement cost as the basis for creating a scalar metric. For example, there might appear to be an underlying assumption that the higher the cost of the total domestic assets associated with a household, the better their living conditions. It also might be assumed that the higher the cost, the more developed the household; consequently, the higher the median value of domestic assets for a community, the more highly developed the community.

Since different cultures place different values on material living conditions, and also on different aspects of these living conditions, such assumptions may distort interpretations in the direction of a Western bias. After all, the scale includes the value of housing, and housing costs involve the costs of such things as bathrooms. Since some houses contain five or six bathrooms, the question arises as to how the number of bathrooms is related to level of development. In other words, how many additional bathrooms are needed to yield an improvement in living conditions or an increase in level of development? The same applies to refrigerators. How fancy a refrigerator is required to improve living conditions? Do people improve their level of social and economic development by having automatic ice and water dispensers on their refrigerators? Such questions can be raised concerning every one of the domestic assets items if we enter a debate over what is meant by better living conditions or higher levels of development. Such a debate brings value issues into the discussion, and such issues are settled only by arbitrary decisions.

This research does *not* make the assumption that higher-cost domestic assets are better or more appropriate than low-cost ones, nor does it assume that high median values of domestic assets represent higher levels of socioeconomic development. Although it provides a means of examining the kinds and value of domestic assets associated with a household, it does so as a means of evaluating disaster losses. No matter how cultures differ in their value orientations, and therefore in the value they place on physical living conditions, the fact remains that high physical impact disasters damage and destroy domestic assets, and these assets have a cost associated with replacement. No matter how they are valued in cultural terms, they remain the means by which the household carries out normal household functions. For these reasons, it does not seem that a Western bias is necessarily associated with this method of measurement when applied to disasters. If the measure is applied in development studies, however, these issues do need to be faced.

Such a bias might enter the picture if we were to rank societies according to their median level of domestic assets and assume that the greater the assets, the more developed the society. Such a ranking assumes that development can be measured by the economic value of physical living conditions. To the extent that this assumption violates the definitions of development based on other value assumptions, it introduces a bias. For example, it ignores the quality of political and civic life, and it entirely ignores aesthetic considerations and spiritual matters.

Similarly, if we were to measure the size or magnitude of a disaster by using the mean level of damage and loss in monetary units such as dollars, it would introduce a bias in favor of richer societies that have inflated values associated with domestic assets. For example, if a random sample of housing units in San Francisco were destroyed, and a similar random sample of houses in Lima were destroyed, and we then took the median value of the housing loss measured in dollars as an index of disaster magnitude, it would appear that the San Francisco disaster was perhaps ten times the magnitude of the one in Lima. In fact, the cost of reconstruction stated in dollars, assuming replacement at local costs, would be different between the two places by a factor somewhere near ten. However, relative to the actual social and economic impact in the sociocultural context of each site, it could be argued that the disasters were of the same magnitude if they resulted in the same proportion of loss to households.

For this reason, disaster magnitude must be measured relative to the base on which disaster impact operates. The best cross-cultural measure, using the Domestic Assets Scale, is therefore one that calculates percentage loss as follows: (Pre-Disaster Assets–Post-Impact Assets)/(Pre-Disaster Assets) x 100. Such a measure evaluates damage and loss against the original investment in domestic assets and therefore results in comparable scores for households in both poor and rich communities. To utilize this scale on the community level, it would, of course, be necessary to use some method to control for the size of the community and for its total investment in domestic assets (Bates and Peacock 1987).

It is important to reemphasize the fact that the Domestic Assets Scale is a measure used at the household level. It evaluates the loss suffered by a single household. It can therefore be used to measure recovery at the household level. To use it at the community level, it is necessary to relate the number of households affected by a disaster to the total number of households in the community and also to the selective nature of the disaster, which is almost always nonrandom.

Even so, the domestic assets technique can be used to estimate the size of the reconstruction task and to estimate the cost of accomplishing it since the scale estimates the replacement cost of domestic assets. To use it for this purpose, however, we must remember that the Domestic Assets Scale does not contain all possible domestic assets items, but only a sample of them. To arrive at the true projected cost of reconstruction, an estimate would be necessary of the proportion of total damage represented by the scale.

Comparisons Based on Exchange Rates and Purchasing Power Parity

Under certain conditions it might be desirable to compare the total monetary value of losses in disasters occurring in countries with different currencies. For example, the international community almost always offers some form of aid to a stricken community. It might therefore be useful to have an estimate of replacement costs convertible into the currency of any country, or even to have an estimate in a kind of international monetary unit.

This study used both standard conversion rates and the purchasing power parity method to calculate the level of domestic assets in six different study communities. The two methods yielded about the same results, using data on the market value of domestic assets items collected *at the time* of the domestic assets survey itself and exchange rates for the same period. This meant that purchasing power parity results were for the same period as the exchange rates, and the relationship between the two was therefore not affected by such things as exchange rate changes or inflation in domestic assets costs.

Following the data collection, however, exchange rates among currencies changed radically, especially in Yugoslavia, Peru, Turkey, and Mexico, relative to the currencies of Italy and the United States. This means that if the figures obtained from the survey were interpreted against today's international monetary situation, they would yield deceptive results. For this reason, comparisons of disasters that occur at different times in different countries using a common currency present serious methodological problems not unlike those associated with comparisons between so-called rich and poor countries. It is suggested that proportion loss be used along with exchange rate, purchasing power parity conversions, and an estimate of the proportion change in exchange rates to arrive at a correction for changes in the relative values of currencies.

Other Uses of the Domestic Assets Technique

Since the Domestic Assets Scale consists of individual measures that gather information on particular items of domestic technology, such as houses, stoves, refrigerators, washing machines, or other items that perform similar functions, item-by-item comparisons are possible. For example, it is possible to compare the types of items damaged or destroyed in earthquakes, floods, and hurricanes. Furthermore, the Domestic Assets Scale can be expanded by adding detailed information on housing characteristics and on the type of damage to dwellings experienced in different types of disasters. In short, the scale is rich in individual items of information and presents the opportunity of focusing on particular aspects of living conditions.

Many items in the Domestic Assets Scale have a direct relationship to health and sanitation. For example, the scale contains items on water supply, human waste disposal, bathing facilities, clothes washing, dishwashing, and cooking facilities. All of these have a potential relationship to health. This means that, in cross-cultural studies not only of disaster reconstruction but of development, it would be possible to use parts of the scale to measure changes in living conditions that have a bearing on health. The Domestic Assets Scale also contains items that can be used to measure dependency on modern energy delivery systems (for example, electric power). Since this is true, the scale likewise can be used to measure the disruption of household functioning in various cultural settings by the loss of energy supply produced by disasters.

The Domestic Assets Scale is a generalized instrument designed to measure living conditions through the gathering of rather detailed information. For this reason, it is a flexible research tool to which items can be added when needed and that can be employed for many purposes in many cultural and economic settings.

Appendix A

Price Data Tables

This appendix contains the price data and conversion ratios used in computing the purchasing power parity conversion ratios discussed in chapter 5.

Table A.1. Prices for Domestic Assets Items

Domestic Assets Items	United States	Italy	Yugoslavia	Mexico	Turkey	Peru
Refrigerator						
Side-by-side						
Ice and water	1,225	4,500,000	30,160,000	—	—	—
Ice maker	800	—	—	—	—	—
No options	700	1,225,000	—	216,349	—	—
Large model						
Ice and water	1,000	—	—	—	—	—
Ice maker	785	78,000	—	—	—	—
No options	620	750,000	271,180	150,098	224,000	8,050,000
Midsize	550	679,500	223,445	109,040	175,000	3,470,000
Compact	205	397,000	132,640	89,311	96,000	2,490,000
Metal ice chest	50	30,000	2,645	14,500	28,500	—
Styrofoam ice chest	4	—	—	—	—	—
Icebox	—	—	—	—	—	—
Food cabinet	—	—	1,885	23,675	—	—
Large freezer	470	450,000	241,050	123,700	—	11,810,000
Small freezer	250	446,000	144,382	93,100	—	—
Full-size range	518	466,250	72,880	62,635	145,500	8,135,750
Self-cleaning	655	534,000	—	—	—	8,135,750
Continuous cleaning	560	—	—	—	—	10,981,500
No cleaning feature	380	398,500	—	—	—	8,000,000

Double range						
Self-cleaning	960	—	—	—	—	—
Smooth cooktop	1,100	—	—	—	—	—
Continuous cleaning	670	—	—	—	—	—
No cleaning feature	630	—	76,450	—	—	—
Microwave-convection						
Self-cleaning	1,030	—	—	—	—	—
Continuous cleaning	935	—	—	—	—	—
Compact range	300	428,750	49,398	57,919	92,000	2,252,500
Self-cleaning	—	526,500	—	—	—	—
Continuous cleaning	—	331,500	—	—	—	—
Single wall oven	463	—	—	—	—	6,400,000
Self-cleaning	555	—	—	—	—	—
Continuous cleaning	380	—	—	—	—	—
No cleaning feature	370	—	—	—	—	—
Double wall oven	628	—	68,500	—	—	—
Self-cleaning	775	—	—	—	—	—
Continuous cleaning	480	—	—	—	—	—
Microwave oven	375	565,000	—	—	650,000	7,137,500
Regular cooktop	225	—	67,947	—	—	3,300,000
Smooth cooktop	370	—	—	—	—	—
Magnetic cooktop	—	—	—	—	—	—
Electric hot plate	38	—	9,486	4,750	16,000	219,000
Toaster oven	50	—	—	—	47,000	—
Charcoal grill	43	—	—	—	—	—
Kerosene stove/oven	—	—	—	—	—	754,800

Table A.1. (*Continued*)

Domestic Assets Items	United States	Italy	Yugoslavia	Mexico	Turkey	Peru
Kerosene oven	—	—	26,648	—	—	—
Iron stove/oven	—	—	24,414	—	30,000	—
Iron stove	—	—	18,440	—	—	—
Clay stove	—	—	—	—	—	—
Formal dining suite	1,025	1,645,500	38,550	233,196	870,000	3,300,000
Kitchen dining suite	250	689,000	18,600	58,863	38,000	—
Secondhand table	—	—	8,614	15,140	—	1,200,000
Informal table	—	—	—	—	—	—
Special platform	—	—	36,595	—	—	—
Box	—	—	0	0	—	0
Pan/tub for clothes washing	10	—	1,162	1,538	600	30,500
Utility sink for clothes washing	59	141,800	16,395	15,442	2,000	—
Nonautomatic clothes washer	—	—	—	41,553	40,000	—
Semiautomatic clothes washer	400	—	—	57,320	135,000	1,666,900
Automatic clothes washer	390	701,300	64,100	93,921	223,000	9,323,000
Automatic dryer	300	400,000	46,480	119,048	—	8,960,000
Electric dishwasher	430	524,000	89,550	190,499	407,000	—
Kitchen sink	215	91,500	15,072	12,367	137,300	817,400
Cement utility sink	59	—	—	—	2,000	—
Pan for dishwashing	—	—	5,617	500	1,150	15,250
King/Queen mattress	695	1,321,000	36,352	45,847	225,000	—

Full/Twin mattress	389	339,000	21,229	37,873	—	1,335,000
Hideaway bed	500	1,756,500	37,530	96,625	125,000	3,384,500
Studio bed	330	688,000	28,305	14,500	85,000	814,500
Roll-away bed	100	116,700	21,700	12,700	19,800	—
Cot	40	52,700	—	6,150	—	180,000
Sleeping pad	—	—	—	5,247	2,750	—
Couch/sofa	—	—	38,550	53,000	—	—
Telephone	40	62,400	16,112	19,637	7,500	—
AM/FM radio	50	63,500	33,005	7,875	7,700	—
AM/FM radio/tape player	135	284,000	31,708	109,000	60,000	2,700,900
Component stereo	1,675	1,734,500	64,250	173,931	476,500	12,597,000
Black/white TV	100	328,500	44,060	52,929	—	988,800
Color TV	435	1,180,000	158,013	215,350	270,000	5,884,900
Console color TV	850	—	—	—	—	—
Large screen TV	1,500	—	—	—	—	—
Video player/recorder	520	1,429,500	227,500	—	307,500	8,712,400
Vacuum cleaner	160	289,000	23,150	48,416	44,500	1,113,000
Carpet sweeper	85	172,000	3,668	—	—	—
Broom	5	8,750	521	352	425	—
Ceiling fan	70	—	24,258	—	—	849,800
Room fan	19	67,500	12,360	16,924	17,000	477,400
Automatic hot water heater	190	161,250	39,341	23,536	130,000	464,500
Pipe hot water heater	—	190,750	10,263	—	—	—
Toilet basin	189	165,250	70,212	81,792	29,750	550,000
Bathroom sink	137	146,100	—	48,966	27,750	—
Bathroom tub	150	260,500	97,111	107,699	53,500	—

Table A.2. Prices Used to Compute Purchasing Power Parity Conversion Ratios

Domestic Assets Items	United States	Italy	Yugoslavia	Mexico	Turkey	Peru
Refrigerator						
Side-by-side						
Ice and water	1,225	4,500,000	—	—	—	30,160,000
Ice maker	700	1,225,000	—	216,349	—	—
Large model	620	750,000	271,180	150,098	224,000	8,050,000
Ice maker	785	778,000	—	—	—	—
Midsize	550	679,500	223,445	109,040	175,000	3,470,000
Compact	205	397,000	132,640	89,311	96,000	2,490,000
Ice chest	50	30,000	2,645	14,500	28,500	—
Large freezer	470	450,000	241,050	123,700	—	11,810,000
Small freezer	250	446,000	144,382	93,100	—	—
Full-size range	518	466,250	72,880	62,635	145,500	8,135,750
Self-cleaning	655	534,000	—	—	—	10,981,500
Continuous cleaning	560	—	—	—	—	8,000,000
No cleaning feature	380	398,500	—	—	—	5,290,000
Double range/regular stove	630	—	764,500	—	—	—
Compact range	300	428,750	49,398	57,919	92,000	2,252,500
Single wall oven	463	—	—	—	—	6,400,000
Double wall oven	628	—	68,500	—	—	—
Microwave oven	375	565,000	—	—	650,000	7,137,500
Regular cooktop	225	—	67,947	—	—	3,300,000

Electric hot plate	38	—	9,486	4,750	16,000	219,000
Toaster oven	50	—	—	—	47,000	—
Formal dining suite	1,025	1,645,500	—	233,196	870,000	—
Kitchen dining suite	250	689,000	18,600	58,863	38,000	—
Pan/tub for dishwashing	10	—	1,162	1,538	600	30,500
Utility sink for clothes washing	59	141,800	16,395	15,442	2,000	—
Semiautomatic clothes washer	400	—	—	57,320	135,000	1,666,900
Automatic clothes washer	390	701,300	64,100	93,921	223,000	9,323,000
Automatic dryer	300	400,000	46,480	119,048	—	8,960,000
Electric dishwasher	430	524,000	89,550	190,499	407,000	—
Kitchen sink	215	91,500	15,072	12,367	137,300	817,400
Cement utility sink	59	—	—	—	2,000	—
King/Queen mattress	695	1,321,000	36,352	45,847	225,000	—
Full/Twin mattress	389	339,000	21,229	37,873	—	1,335,000
Hideaway bed	500	1,756,500	37,530	96,625	125,000	3,384,500
Studio bed	330	688,000	28,305	14,500	85,000	814,500
Roll-away bed	100	116,700	21,700	12,700	19,800	—
Cot	40	52,700	—	6,150	—	180,000
Telephone	40	62,400	16,112	19,637	7,500	—
AM/FM radio	50	63,500	33,005	7,875	7,700	—
AM/FM radio/tape player	135	284,000	31,708	109,000	60,000	2,700,900
Black/white TV	100	328,500	44,060	52,929	—	988,800
Color TV	435	1,180,000	158,013	215,350	270,000	5,884,900
Video player/recorder	520	1,429,500	227,500	—	307,500	8,712,400
Vacuum cleaner	160	289,000	23,150	48,416	44,500	1,113,000
Rug/room sweeper	85	172,000	3,668	—	—	—

Table A.2. (*Continued*)

Domestic Assets Items	United States	Italy	Yugoslavia	Mexico	Turkey	Peru
Broom	5	8,750	521	352	425	—
Ceiling fan	70	—	24,258	—	—	849,800
Room fan	19	67,500	12,360	16,924	17,000	477,400
Automatic hot water heater	190	161,250	39,341	23,536	130,000	464,500
Toilet	189	165,250	70,212	81,792	29,750	550,000
Porcelain bathroom sink	137	146,100	—	48,966	27,750	—
Bathroom tub	150	260,500	97,111	107,699	53,500	—

Table A.3. Purchasing Power Parity Ratios for Each Domestic Asset Item

Domestic Assets Items	Italy/U.S.	Yugoslavia/U.S.	Mexico/U.S.	Turkey/U.S.	Peru/U.S.
Refrigerator					
Side-by-side					
Ice and water	3,673.469	—	—	—	24,620.408
Ice maker	1,750.000	—	309.070	—	—
Large model	1,209.677	437.387	242.094	361.290	12,983.871
Ice maker	991.083	—	—	—	—
Midsize	1,235.455	406.264	198.255	318.182	6,309.091
Compact	1,936.585	647.024	435.663	468.293	12,146.341
Ice chest	600.000	52.900	290.000	570.000	—
Large freezer	957.447	512.872	263.191	—	25,127.660
Small freezer	784.000	577.528	372.400	—	—
Full-size range	900.097	140.695	120.917	280.888	15,706.081
Self-cleaning	815.267	—	—	—	16,765.649
Continuous cleaning	—	—	—	—	14,285.714
No cleaning feature	1,048.684	—	—	—	13,921.053
Double range/regular stove	—	121.349	—	—	—
Compact range	1,429.167	164.660	193.063	306.667	7,508.333
Single wall oven	—	—	—	—	13,822.894
Double wall oven	—	109.076	—	—	—
Microwave oven	506.667	—	—	1733.333	19,033.333
Regular cooktop	—	301.987	—	—	14,666.667
Electric hot plate	—	249.632	125.000	421.053	5,763.158

Table A.3. (*Continued*)

Domestic Assets Items	Italy/U.S.	Yugoslavia/U.S.	Mexico/U.S.	Turkey/U.S.	Peru/U.S.
Toaster oven	—	—	—	940.000	—
Formal dining suite	1,605.366	—	227.508	848.780	—
Kitchen dining suite	2,756.000	74.400	235.452	152.000	—
Pan/tub for dishwashing	—	116.200	153.800	60.000	3,050.000
Utility sink for clothes washing	2,403.390	277.881	261.729	33.898	—
Semiautomatic clothes washer	—	—	143.300	337.500	4,167.250
Automatic clothes washer	1,798.205	164.359	240.823	571.795	23,905.128
Automatic dryer	1,333.333	154.933	396.827	—	29,866.667
Electric dishwasher	1,218.605	208.256	443.021	946.512	—
Kitchen sink	425.581	70.102	57.521	638.605	3,801.860
Cement utility sink	—	—	—	33.898	—
King/Queen mattress	1,900.719	52.305	65.967	323.741	—
Full/Twin mattress	871.465	54.573	97.360	—	3,431.877
Hideaway bed	3,513.000	75.060	193.250	250.000	6,769.000
Studio bed	2,084.848	85.773	43.939	257.576	2,468.182
Roll-away bed	1,167.000	217.000	127.000	198.000	—
Cot	1,317.500	—	153.750	—	4,500.000
Telephone	1,560.000	402.800	490.925	187.500	—
AM/FM radio	1,270.000	660.100	157.500	154.000	—
AM/FM radio/tape player	2,103.704	234.874	807.407	444.444	20,006.667
Black/white TV	3,285.000	440.600	529.290	—	9,888.000

Color TV	2,712.644	363.248	495.057	620.690	13,528.506
Video player/recorder	2,749.038	437.500	—	591.346	16,754.615
Vacuum cleaner	1,806.250	144.688	302.600	278.125	6,956.250
Rug/room sweeper	2,023.529	43.153	—	—	—
Broom	1,750.000	104.200	70.400	85.000	—
Ceiling fan	—	346.543	—	—	12,140.000
Room fan	3,552.632	650.526	890.737	894.737	25,126.316
Automatic hot water heater	848.684	207.058	123.874	684.211	2,444.737
Toilet	874.339	371.492	432.762	157.407	2,910.053
Porcelain bathroom sink	1,066.423	—	357.416	202.555	—
Bathroom tub	1,736.667	647.407	717.993	356.667	—

Commentaries on the Domestic
Assets Approach

Two members of the international research team that conducted this research were asked to submit critical comments concerning the results. These comments were to be directed especially toward the question of the cross-cultural utility of the Domestic Assets Scale. It should be noted that, taking these comments into account, some changes were subsequently made to the book. Nevertheless, these comments have been included here for the reader's use in assessing the research's strengths and weaknesses.

Commentary on the Domestic Assets Method for
Measuring Disaster Impact (Aydin Germen, Turkey)

This study, which represents a confluence of many past strands of research in American sociology, can be fruitfully expanded in several directions in the future. In its choice of subject matter, in its curiosity about details concerning ways of living, and in some of its treatments and findings, I have found the study, in my personal capacity as a city planner, decidedly "sweet," this being the highest praise.

The investigation of household implements and amenities seems to provide a more significant, and inferentially more tangible, basis in evidence than many other types of community studies. For example, a diagnostic and predictive sociological study of Söke's neighbor city, Kusadasi, conducted in the 1960s, proved totally false within five years of its publication. Other studies that have focused on the statistics of primary education and on readership of qualitatively different newspapers have been trivial and have led to unwarranted conclusions.

Although there have not been many sociological studies of community structure or power structure in Turkey, international newspaper reports have seemed more incisive than the social science studies that have been produced. In contrast, information on the distribution of domestic assets, and on the variety of occupations and professions obtained from this study, provide a very lively picture of Söke, mainly by inference, but such inferences appear more trust-worthy than direct studies of structure or power. If and when occupations and professions, and other ways of living and making a living, are not reduced to code numbers, but are observed in their lateral connections, the picture of a town will be livelier still.

The overall methodology for this study, however, will be more fruitful if it is divested of its dependence on valuation scales, from excessive interest in status analysis, from national frameworks and comparisons, from a trust in the precision of international monetary equivalences, and from emphasizing theoretical considerations over discrete field findings, whether or not these approaches are often adopted in social and economic studies. In the following, I shall be content to list major themes and refrain as much as possible from detailed discussions.

Commentary on International Comparisons

This study assumed a continuum in the assets scales from one community to the other, and the researchers tried to extend the scale to the uppermost and lowermost limits in a reasonable way. Since application of this study's scale is actually not continuous with respect to sample communities or countries, the findings should be treated as discrete cells, and we should take care not to use the word stochastic. Perhaps the findings should not even be presented in matrix form if that form implies the relative ranking of countries.

In this study, the scaling of assets was topped by cities and, in turn, by the scaling of countries. The thing to do in this case is to strike out country names from the analyses since the communities chosen for study do not represent the countries from which they came, and the study's methodology does not require them to do so. A more restrictive frame also suits disaster studies for which this domestic assets scale was developed, since disasters take place at local or district levels.

To illustrate the inappropriateness of country comparisons, Udine was selected in Italy in terms of suitability and convenience for research, as was the case with cities in other countries. But the much higher income in Italy in recent years, joined with Udine's relative place in the Italian political economy, will produce biased impressions in the findings, especially if lower-ranked regions are selected in other countries that have lower average incomes than Italy. But Udine is not, by far, the major offender with respect to nonrepresentativeness in this study. If I remember correctly, Santa Barbara is the fourth richest county in the United States. Since countless other U.S. towns could provide figures on the possession of the uppermost level of domestic assets items, what we get from data obtained in Santa Barbara is the following: How does a well-to-do community distribute its financial resources on the upper and lower ends of the Domestic Assets Scale? Now, if this information by-produces lopsidedness and bias in the interpretation of the overall results, the lesson to be drawn is not to exclude Santa Barbara, but to refrain from overreaching in conclusions and correlations by extending them to national comparisons.

If we take Söke in comparison with Santa Barbara, the two towns certainly share a few traits, such as a Mediterranean climate and the arrival of the railway in nearly the same year. But Söke certainly is not situated within its country's political economy in the way that Santa Barbara is in its own. Agreed that our study has excluded data on local rarities such as diamonds and the like from the uppermost end of the scale (thus, Santa Barbara cannot show its own extra luxury items), still the California city has further characteristics to distinguish it from the others. For example, it is one of the few cities on earth that were very much spruced up after a disaster. This followed the 1925 earthquake. At the point where the study ramifies into national frames, value continua, and especially status considerations, these subjects that themselves should undergo highly critical scrutiny instead dominate the assets list and introduce difficulties in omission and commission.

Take, for example, the most expensive type of refrigerator, which dispenses water like an Italian garden statuette, and ice like W. C. Fields on a snowy mountain. This, of course, is a commodity, but if one wants to ask, "What do people do with the energy they save thanks to such a refrigerator?," one should not be faced with accepting the sanction given to the implement by the assets survey. Such a matter is the subject of other sociological studies. Or, take beds. In terms of either technological improvement, or in terms of the assets value scale, perhaps the quality of the mattress should precede any other consideration. But when we start from king-size beds and go eventually to cots and floor pads, the question of spurious status, or of gimmicks, presents itself. Again, these questions are themselves subjects for sociological inquiry.

When the above considerations are compounded with continua that rank nations, the questions become even more complicated. But there may be surprises either way, we must admit. With respect to the expensive refrigerator, for instance, we had proposed its exclusion from the assets list on the grounds that no similar refrigerator was likely to be found in Turkey at that time, so why search for it? When the group's principal investigator visited Izmir next morning, he took me to see exactly such a refrigerator on the esplanade, and he had not yet seen one in the country for which the item was included in the list.

In this inquiry, implement (domestic asset) value and social status have a continual entry and exit in the framework against each other. But they are certainly not equivalent. The gimmick or novelty value of an item is not a basic quality of domestic assets. The monetary weighting of assets is certainly more to the point than arbitrary ranking scales. But monetary weighting has its own deficiencies, monetary imprecision in the international frame being one. Another is that some items are of expressed market value, whereas it is next to impossible or undesirable to do so for housing, when the concern is postdisaster replacement and when this is to be expressed internationally.

Social status as a criterion stands against technical efficiency as well. Efficiency itself is not likely to be a satisfactory measure: first, because it may not be what it is presented to be; second, because its measures will be lost inside those of marketing and market value; and last, because it will not invariantly be proportional to cost and value scales.

The above two paragraphs present a few complete, intermeshed circles of argument. Perhaps the thing to do is to sieve the items to be included, with respect to their replacement cost, often without common formal criteria, through a performance evaluation of the items. This should not be impossible in the present circumstances. This seems to provide better criteria for replacing technical efficiency and does not depend on social status, for instance.

The examples of mattresses and refrigerators were used. We should be able to take to task other questions, such as a hypothetical guest bedroom used for no other purpose? Information obtained in this respect would, of course, be quite valuable in more than one respect, and it would serve for a social critique as well, but once it gets summed up on a monetary or other scale it vitiates the purpose of classical Japanese architecture, much of sober rural architecture, and many contemporary architectural theorists by imputing top asset values to such an arrangement. Let us consider a second phone for a dwelling unit. It is a negligible asset, and a negligible investment. If, then, it measures anything, does it point to status, or information, or convenience? Is it more of a convenience, or an inconvenience? Is it correct to assume that, at the least, a second phone measures communication? How much is a second phone—or a single one, for that matter—a measure of misinformation? An assets survey must not make any assumptions, explicit or implicit, in these respects. Instead, such matters should be left to studies of time spent using telephones in metropolitan areas, without even getting into communication, there already being frightful statistics on this subject (e.g., New York City).

Questions of this nature came up in the study group's initial discussions. For instance, if a region does not really need much air-conditioning, is a region in need of it automatically to be considered superior because it exhibits additional expensive items? It is not when we consider such queries, but when we neglect them, that we pass on to connotations beyond disaster impact and assets evaluation.

One other account that prompts me to make these remarks concerns postdisaster claims. Our own earthquake experiences have led to a disbelief in such claims. It is also well-known that in a postdisaster phase, much material is mislaid and much graft takes place. Our study in its present form will be very valuable in estimating recovery rates, but as a pioneer study it should not become the model for claims forms.

As a last general question, we may ask, "In what respect may the international context be expressed in terms of a national and cross-cultural comparison framework?" Let us consider the national frame first. We should be careful of cross-national comparisons because the measures are not very common cross-nationally. Even on the simplest level and for items concerning which international value attribution is on the ascendancy, questions of the following nature will crop up: Among the most fashionable refrigerators of several countries, which one will top the international list?

I have made clear my objections to a national framework of analysis in contrast to a community-based one, although in my country this would be next to impossible for certain items and very difficult and unpleasant work for others. As it is, we did obtain most prices for domestic assets at the national level. These included prices for items not found in Söke, and consequently not included in the final international list of monetary comparisons, but found in the Izmir and Istanbul markets; it also included items from the lowermost spectrum, generally purchased by households in the past, quoted prices not being easily available in Söke, but found in the larger cities.

Construction costs for housing units will be more readily available nationally. On the other hand, my experience as a city planner and economist is that members of concerned professions are reluctant to venture costs per specific building types of the nature we had specified in our study, and the knowledge that given international bodies had not come forward with a cost-accounting scheme that could be used generally, let alone internationally, has made us suspect the validity of the figures to be obtained. This defect does not necessarily defeat the present study's purpose, but it does cast doubts on its precision. An internationally valid building cost estimation scheme remains to be put on some agenda. The components approach from the United Kingdom does not seem to have made much headway.

The above difficulties in themselves are at odds with the intentions of cross-cultural surveys. But when we have research intentions on an international level, and then attempt to express the findings quantitatively, there may be other factors that defeat rigorous handling. A case in point concerns the percentage of the sample drawn according to status sectors. In Turkey, 10.1 percent of the sample was in the high-status sectors, while the figure was 16.1 percent in the United States (the status of a housing area or sampling sector being defined in terms of each country itself). In Italy, this figure was 27.4 percent, in Mexico, 23.1 percent. Medium status was represented by 69.3 and 61.7 percent in the United States and in Italy, while it was 27.8 percent in Turkey. Low-status figures were Italy, 10.9; the United States, 14.6; Yugoslavia, 52.5; and Turkey, 62.1 percent. This situation makes up a fourth factor toward an upper-scale-oriented bias. Once more it is valuable information, but to proceed with these figures and furthermore establish correspondences with other figures is really not methodologically necessary in an assets study, and not suitable for comparative analysis.

At this point I perhaps should mention the havoc created by inflation in 1989, making a rechecking of prices nearly meaningless. Of the six countries involved, through the communities selected, Turkey with some 70 percent annual inflation was a distant and more fortunate fourth. One need not mention the figures for the three other countries, but this situation itself points to future difficulties of cross-cultural studies and suggests that some of the precision assumptions be dropped. Even so, the studies will still be fruitful.

The cross-cultural approach is, of course, a welcome corrective to previous work in this field, and it originated from significant and weighty field experience. Some questions, however, remain. For example, what is a cross-cultural inquiry, and how cross-cultural may it be in a generalized, standardized, and quantified scheme of analysis?

My own impression of the subject matter of cross-cultural studies can be formally defined as follows: What is comprehensible from the premises of one culture to another? What is incompatible from one set of premises to another? A common framework for the cross-cultural study ignores by definition the incompatible premises and, unless the researchers are very careful, will use the premises of one culture rather than those extendable across cultures. Ideologically neutral items such as implements, as we may like to think in our more optimistic moments, may be more effectively studied between cultures, but any rankings or average or median values between and among samples from different cultural settings again will assume incompatible premises as being compatible.

In present-day Turkey, the inhabitants of rural areas face mottoes in English during political meetings, journalists with substandard Turkish write the concluding lines of their jokes in substandard English, names of ships and goods are in English, all of these with a smattering of other languages and a good deal of Turkish. Marketing depends on extra-cultural contexts, and prices have gone international since 1985 by fiat rather than by supply-and-demand adjustments. Turkish people and the media supply news of their own culture using unassimilated foreign words, and therefore nothing is intelligible or intelligent according to older reference points, or to new ones. The exchange of ideas and goods does not take place between countries—say, India and Turkey—except through the mediation of a few others. And zombie expressiveness is universal. Whatever culture dominates people today will soon be dominated by these acolytes.

Under these circumstances, it may be quite out of place to speak of distinct cultures. However, if this is the present situation, comparative studies among communities are not cross-cultural. On the other hand, assumptions or the lack of them with respect to the distinct premises that possibly can be found in different communities constantly bring cross-cultural dilemmas to the surface. The remarkable effort made by the Athens, Georgia, group in compiling a list of an international variety of goods at the lower end of the economic scale, following the presuppositions implicit in the scale itself as to progress and development, does not provide a list of cross-cultural variety as much as it points to a list of items likely to disappear soon. When we come to this point, we realize that the cross-cultural framework used in this research has actually been a brave one, but the expression of perhaps independent values in a single continuum serves on the contrary the purposes of whatever is obliterating cultural variety.

Summing up, my attitudes on the methodological content of this study may have been influenced by considerations of city planning and disaster response, but they also suggest that in the future the requirements of the subject matter itself should take precedence over traditional theoretical frames of sociology, and of economics. For the present, caution should be used with respect to the following matters:

1. On *international monetary measurements,* the present rates of inflation in many countries introduce an element of the unreal, even in the national framework, let alone the international one. As an example, while this was being written I came across a newspaper headline, "Schools Will Now Cost 15 Million." As a first reaction, I say, "So construction cost has now gone up to 15 million." It takes a few seconds to realize that the above refers only to the annual costs of educating a single student. In Turkey, there have been serious discussions that Turkish national income per capita is around $4,000 per year, rather than about $1,250 as estimated by the World Bank. We take this debate seriously. Internationally, monetary exchange rates are mainly conveniences

for business circles, and sometimes very serious inconveniences for the same circles. Seven or eight factors may affect these rates, and when one of them goes critical (and an initial adjustment is made by fiat), the values of all the others are affected, thus introducing an element of arbitrariness into production and purchase values.

2. On *development assumptions,* monetary values, although superior to arbitrary ranking values, will hide much more significant processes. As an example, monetary statistics may show a phenomenal rate of urbanization for Turkey over past decades, but they will hide the sad decline in construction quality per given markets, a much more important datum. The so-called developing countries of the world, or at least many of them, should instead be thought of as entities increasingly unable to cope with more recent business conditions, and especially with their population increases. In a series of meetings on nanotechnology at the Massachusetts Institute of Technology in January 1989, the possible effects of this cornucopia were discussed. The tone-setter of the meeting, a very optimistic person, said that we should expect some of the more advanced developments to take place a hundred years from now. Even so, I read that some of these developments are being attempted at present. At the 1989 meeting, there were also comments that plenty and leisure are proportionally linked to violence. All assumptions relating to development should be tempered with either of these two comments.

I notice from our study that Santa Barbara lags far behind the other five towns surveyed in clothes washing equipment, 36 percent of Santa Barbara's households not having any and most likely using laundromats or other facilities. My approach to the sociological interpretation of the assets scale is that this fact represents advance and not retardation, and therefore in my mind makes Santa Barbara more distinctive than any other item included on the Domestic Assets Scale.

Santa Barbara, probably a legendary personality, has been assigned by many people to a city only some hours by present travel standards away from Söke. It was this saint's job to safeguard people and assets from thunderstorms. She should now concentrate on other disasters and, if possible, provide us with fewer assets with more and direct functions.

Commentary on the Domestic Assets Scale as a Measure of Disaster Impact (Carlo Pelanda, Italy)

The Domestic Assets Scale developed in this study must be understood as a research instrument that generates a particular, and limited, image of one aspect of social reality. It focuses the observer's attention on physical living conditions as they apply within households, and it completely ignores other characteristics of households and their living conditions. For example, it supplies no information on the aesthetic or cultural dimensions of living conditions, nor does it offer anything concerning the living conditions that surround the household in the community. It also ignores the relative cultural or psychological values held by household members with respect to particular dimensions of living conditions.

Since it uses monetary weights to arrive at a quantitative score, it emphasizes the economic value or monetary costs of domestic assets. By so doing, it ignores their qualitative characteristics as well as the relative importance of particular items of material culture to physical living conditions. Furthermore, it does not deal with the importance of physical living conditions compared to other dimensions of life within the household. A household's score therefore reflects only the economic value of items that make up the household's living conditions and does not necessarily indicate how well these items function to meet household needs or to satisfy cultural values and aspirations.

This characteristic of creating a particularized and restricted image of social reality is shared with any measuring instrument, since each measure inevitably selects only part of the data available from a phenomenological domain and places these data into a theoretical context that creates a "restricted," or "bounded," image of reality generated by the methodology employed. In this case, since its various items are highly intercorrelated, the scale does have the merit of being based on a set of clearly defined items that appear to have internal consistency. The scale also has the characteristic of dealing with a phenomenon, "living conditions," which is ordinarily affected in disasters and which is involved in post-disaster reconstruction.

Because of its limited nature, caution is called for in expanding interpretations of the results of the Domestic Assets Scale beyond its restricted realm of measurement. The scale has the capacity to measure physical losses suffered by individual households in various cultural settings and of monitoring progress in reconstructing physical living conditions at the household level. To measure the magnitude of a disaster at the community level in terms of impact on living conditions, it will be necessary to find a way of relating the number of households experiencing damage and loss from impact to the total number of households exposed to the disaster.

With respect to cross-cultural comparisons, some difficulties stem from the use of monetary weights, which make it advisable to base such comparisons on percentage loss rather than on the absolute monetary value of the loss. Because of fluctuations in exchange rates and because of varying rates of inflation in various countries at various times, absolute cost comparisons will always remain difficult to interpret and will often be misleading. In addition, difficulties may be experienced in measuring progress toward recovery using monetary weights if price inflation severely affects the cost of domestic assets items during the recovery process. This means that estimates of recovery using this scale must take into account the inflation rate. It is assumed that recovery would be defined as the replacement of lost domestic assets with comparable assets. After inflation, the same set of domestic assets items would cost more, and one might be led to conclude that a positive economic advance and not mere recovery had taken place.

In general, the Domestic Assets Scale, used with proper caution, should nevertheless prove to be a valuable resource for cross-cultural studies, and it should provide a means of comparing the relative impact of various types of disasters on living conditions.

Bibliography

Abril-Ojeda, Galo. 1982. *The Role of Disaster Relief for Long-Term Development in LDCs*. Stockholm: University of Stockholm, Institute of Latin American Studies.

Ad hoc Committee. 1956. Sociological Research in Rural Levels and Standards of Living. *Rural Sociology* 21:183–95.

Andrews, Frank M., ed. 1986. *Research on the Quality of Life*. Ann Arbor, Mich.: Survey Research Center, Institute for Social Research.

Baker, George W., and Dwight W. Chapman. 1962. *Man and Society in Disaster*. New York: Basic Books.

Balassa, Bela. 1964. The Purchasing Power Parity Doctrine: A Reappraisal. *Journal of Political Economy* 72:584–96.

Barton, Allen H. 1963. *Social Organization under Stress*. Washington, D.C.: National Academy of Sciences—National Research Council.

Bates, Frederick L., ed. 1982. *Recovery, Change and Development: A Longitudinal Study of the Guatemalan Earthquake*. Athens, Ga.: Department of Sociology, University of Georgia.

Bates, Frederick L., Timothy Farrell, and JoAnn K. Glittenberg. 1979. Some Changes in Housing Characteristics Following the 1976 Earthquake and Their Implications for Future Earthquake Vulnerability. *Mass Emergencies* 4:121–33.

Bates, Frederick L., C. W. Foglemen, V. J. Parenton, R. H. Pittman, and G. S. Tracy. 1963. *The Social and Psychological Consequences of a Natural Disaster: A Longitudinal Study of Hurricane Audrey*. Washington, D.C.: National Academy of Sciences, National Research Council. Disaster Study No. 18.

Bates, Frederick L., and Charles D. Killian. 1981. The Effects of the 1976 Guatemalan Earthquake on Earthen Houses in Guatemala. In *International Workshop on Earthen Buildings in Seismic Areas*, edited by Gerald W. May, 229–46. Albuquerque: University of New Mexico Press.

Bates, Frederick L., Charles D. Killian, and Walter Gillis Peacock. 1984. An Assessment of Impact and Recovery at the Household Level. *Journal of Ekistics* 51(308): 439–45.

Bates, Frederick L., and Walter Gillis Peacock. 1987. Disasters and Social Change. In *The Sociology of Disasters*, edited by Russell R. Dynes, B. De Marchi, and Carlo Pelanda, 291–330. Gorizia, Italy: Franco Angeli Press.

————. 1989. Long Term Recovery. *International Journal of Mass Emergencies and Disasters* 7(3):349–65.

————. 1992. Measuring Disaster Impact on Household Living Conditions: The Domestic Assets Approach. *International Journal of Mass Emergencies and Disasters* 10(1):133–60.

Belcher, John C. 1972. A Cross-Cultural Household Level of Living Scale. *Rural Sociology* 37(2):208–20.

Berry, Charles R. 1981. *The Reform in Oaxaca, 1956–76: A Microhistory of the Liberal Revolution.* Lincoln: University of Nebraska Press.

Blanton, Richard E. 1979. *Monte Alban: Settlement Patterns at the Ancient Zapotec Capital.* New York: Academic Press.

Bolin, Robert C. 1976. Family Recovery from Natural Disaster: A Preliminary Model. *Mass Emergencies* 1:267–77.

————. 1982. *Long-term Family Recovery from Disaster.* Boulder: University of Colorado, Institute of Behavioral Science, Program on Environment and Behavior, Monograph No. 36.

Bolin, Robert C., and Patricia A. Bolton. 1983. Recovery in Nicaragua and the USA. *International Journal of Mass Emergencies and Disasters* 1:125–44.

Bolin, Robert C., and Patricia Trainer. 1978. Modes of Family Recovery Following Disaster: A Cross-National Study. In *Disasters: Theory and Research*, edited by Enrico L. Quarantelli, 233–47. Beverly Hills: Sage.

Boulding, Kenneth E. 1984. *The Economics of Human Betterment.* Albany: State University of New York Press.

Brown, Lester R., ed. 1990. *State of the World, 1990.* New York: W. W. Norton.

————. 1991a. *State of the World, 1991.* New York: W. W. Norton.

————. 1991b. *The World Watch Reader: On Global and Environmental Issues.* New York: W. W. Norton.

————. 1992. *State of the World, 1992.* New York: W. W. Norton.

Carmines, Edward A., and Richard A. Zeller. 1979. *Reliability and Validity Assessment.* Beverly Hills: Sage.

Change, John K. 1976. The Urban Indian in Colonial Oaxaca. *American Ethnologist* 3(4):610.

————. 1978. *Race and Class in Colonial Oaxaca.* Stanford, Calif.: Stanford University Press.

Chapin, F. Stuart. 1938. *The Measurement of Socio-Economic Status.* Minneapolis: University of Minnesota Press.

Cronbach, L. J. 1951. Coefficient Alpha and the Internal Structure of Test. *Psychometrika* 16:297–334.

Cronbach, L. J., and P. E. Meehl. 1955. Construct Validity in Psychological Tests. *Psychological Bulletin* 52:281–334.

Di Sopra, Luciano. 1986. *Impact Magnitude.* Gorizia, Italy: Franco Angeli.

Drabek, Thomas E. 1986. *Human System Responses to Disaster.* New York: Springer-Verlag.

Drewnowski, Jan. 1970. *Studies in the Measurements of Levels of Living and Welfare*. Report No. 70.3 (Unrisd/70/c.20). Geneva: United Nations Research Institute for Social Development.

Durning, Alan Thein, and Holly B. Brough. 1992. Reforming the Livestock Economy. In *State of the World, 1992*, edited by Lester R. Brown, 66–82. New York: W. W. Norton.

Esparza, Manuel. 1983. *Padron de Capitacion de la Ciudad de Oaxaca, 1875*. Oaxaca: Archivo General del Estado de Oaxaca.

Flavin, Christopher. 1991. The Heat Is On. In *The World Watch Reader*, edited by Lester R. Brown, 75–94. New York: W. W. Norton.

Friesema, H. Paul, James Caporaso, Gerald Goldstein, Robert Lineberry, and Richard McCleary. 1979. *Aftermath: Communities after Natural Disasters*. Beverly Hills: Sage.

Fritz, Charles E. 1961. Disasters. In *Contemporary Social Problems*, edited by Robert K. Merton and Robert A. Nisbet, 651–94. New York: Harcourt, Brace and World.

Hagood, Margaret Jarman, and Louis J. Ducoff. 1944. What Level of Living Indexes Measure. *American Sociological Review* 9:78–84.

Hill, Ruben, and Donald A. Hansen. 1962. Families in Disaster. In *Man and Society in Disaster*, edited by George W. Baker and Dwight W. Chapman, 185–221. New York: Basic Books.

Hoover, Greg A., and Frederick L. Bates. 1985. The Impact of a Natural Disaster on the Division of Labor in Twelve Guatemalan Communities: A Study of Social Change in a Developing Country. *International Journal of Mass Emergencies and Disasters* 3(3):9–26.

Hultåker, Örjan, and Jan Trost, eds. 1983. Family and Disasters. *The International Journal of Mass Emergencies and Disasters* 1:1–128.

Katzner, Donald W. 1979. *Choice and the Quality of Life*. Beverly Hills: Sage.

Killian, Charles D., and Frederick L. Bates. 1982. An Assessment of Impact and Recovery at the Household Level. In *Recovery, Change and Development: A Longitudinal Study of the Guatemalan Earthquake*, edited by Frederick L. Bates, 731–91. Athens, Ga.: Department of Sociology, University of Georgia.

Killian, Charles D., Walter Gillis Peacock, and Frederick L. Bates. 1982. A Multivariate Analysis of Factors Affecting Earthquake Recovery. In *Recovery, Change and Development: A Longitudinal Study of the Guatemalan Earthquake*, edited by Frederick L. Bates, 893–906. Athens, Ga.: Department of Sociology, University of Georgia.

———. 1983. The Impact of the 1976 Guatemalan Earthquake on Inequality of Household Domestic Assets. Paper presented at the Midwestern Sociological Society's annual meetings, Kansas City, Mo.

———. 1984. Decomposing Inequality Trends Following the 1976 Guatemalan Earthquake. Paper presented at the Southern Sociological Society's annual meetings, Knoxville, Tenn.

Knox, Paul L. 1974. Social Indicators and the Concept of Level of Living. *Sociological Review* 22(2):249–57.

Kravis, Irving B., Allen W. Heston, and Robert Summers. 1978a. *International Comparison of National Products and Purchasing Power*. Baltimore: Johns Hopkins University Press.

———. 1978b. Real GDP Per Capita for More Than One Hundred Countries. *Review of Income and Wealth* 27:33–55.

———. 1982. *World Product and Income: International Comparisons of Real Gross Products*. Baltimore: Johns Hopkins University Press.

Kreps, Gary A. 1984. Sociological Inquiry and Disaster Research. *Annual Review of Sociology* 10:309–30.

Lenski, Gerhard E. 1966. *Power and Privilege*. New York: McGraw-Hill.

Lenski, Gerhard E., Jean Lenski, and Patrick Nolan. 1991. *Human Societies*. New York: McGraw-Hill.

Mileti, Dennis S. 1987. Sociological Methods and Disaster Research. In *The Sociology of Disasters*, edited by Russell R. Dynes, B. De Marchi, and Carlo Pelanda, 57–69. Gorizia, Italy: Franco Angeli Press.

Mileti, Dennis S., Thomas E. Drabek, and H. Eugene Haas. 1975. *Human Systems in Extreme Environments: A Sociological Perspective*. Boulder: University of Colorado, Institute of Behavioral Science, Program on Environment and Behavior, Monograph No. 21.

Morris, Morris David. 1979. *Measuring the Condition of the World's Poor: The Physical Quality of Life Index*. New York: Pergamon Press.

Murphy, Arthur D. 1985. Studying Housing Areas in a Developing Nation: Lessons from Oaxaca City, Mexico. *Housing and Society* 14(2):143–60.

Murphy, Arthur D., and Alex Stepick. 1991. *Adaptation and Inequality in Oaxaca: Political Economy and Cultural Ecology in an Intermediate Mexican City*. Austin: University of Texas Press.

Nolasco, Margarita. 1981. *Cuatro Ciudades: El Proceso de Urbanizacion Dependiente*. Mexico: INAH.

Peacock, Walter Gillis, and Frederick L. Bates. 1982. Ethnic Differences in Earthquake Impact and Recovery. In *Recovery, Change and Development: A Longitudinal Study of the Guatemalan Earthquake*, edited by Frederick L. Bates, 792–892. Athens, Ga.: Department of Sociology, University of Georgia.

Peacock, Walter Gillis, Charles D. Killian, and Frederick L. Bates. 1987. The Effects of Disaster Damage and Housing Aid on Household Recovery Following the 1976 Guatemalan Earthquake. *International Journal of Mass Emergencies and Disasters* 5:63–88.

Peacock, Walter Gillis, Charles D. Killian, Greg A. Hoover, and Frederick L. Bates. 1984. Alterations in Community Complexity and Household Recovery Following the 1976 Guatemalan Earthquake. Paper presented at the American Sociological Association's annual meetings, San Antonio, Texas.

Peacock, Walter Gillis, Greg A. Hoover, and Charles D. Killian. 1988. Divergence and Convergence in International Development: A Decomposition Analysis of Inequality in the World System. *American Sociological Review* 53:838–52.

Postel, Sandra, and John C. Rayan. 1991. Reforming Forestry. In *State of the World, 1991*, edited by Lester Brown, 74–92. New York: W. W. Norton.

Prince, Samuel H. 1925. *Catastrophe and Social Change*. New York: Columbia University Press.

Quarantelli, Enrico L. 1978. *Disasters: Theory and Research*. Beverly Hills: Sage.

Ramsey, Charles E., and Jenaro Collazo. 1960. Some Problems of Cross-Cultural Measurement. *Rural Sociology* 25(1):91–106.

Rodeheaver, Daniel Gilbert. 1990. Household Internal Structure and Composition, Social Context and Domestic Assets Accumulation and Reaccumulation Following a Disaster: The 1976 Guatemalan Earthquake. Ph.D. dissertation. Department of Sociology: University of Georgia.

Selby, Henry A., Arthur D. Murphy, and Steve Lorenzen. In press. *The Mexican Urban Household: Organizing for Self-Defense*. Austin: University of Texas Press.

Sewell, William H. 1940. A Scale for the Measurement of Farm Family Socioeconomic Status. *Southwestern Social Science Quarterly* 21(2):125–37.

———. 1943. The Restandardization of a Sociometric Scale. *Social Forces* 21: 302–11.

Sharp, Emmit F., and Charles E. Ramsey. 1963. Criteria of Item Selection in Level of Living Scales. *Rural Sociology* 28(2):146–64.

Simpson, Eyler N. 1937. *The Ejido: Mexico's Way Out*. Chapel Hill: University of North Carolina Press.

Sobel, Michael E. 1981. *Lifestyle and Social Structure: Concepts, Definitions, and Analyses*. New York: Academic Press.

———. 1983. Lifestyle Differentiation and Stratification in Contemporary U.S. Society. *Research in Social Stratification and Mobility* 2:115–44.

Summers, Robert, and Alan Heston. 1984. Improved International Comparisons of Real Product and Its Composition, 1950–80. *Review of Income and Wealth* 30:207–62.

———. 1988. A New Set of International Comparisons of Real Product and Price Level Estimates for 130 Countries, 1950–1985. *Review of Income and Wealth* 34:1–25.

Summers, Robert, Irving B. Kravis, and Alan Heston. 1980. International Comparisons of Real Product and Its Composition: 1950–77. *Review of Income and Wealth* 26:19–66.

Terleckyj, N. E. 1975. *Improvements in the Quality of Life: Estimates of the Possibilities in the United States, 1974–83*. Washington, D.C.: National Planning Association.

Ugalde, Antonio. 1970. Measuring Wealth in a Semi-Cash Economy. *Rural Sociology* 28(4):146–64.

UN Report. 1953. *Definition and Measurement of Standards of Living*. Chicago: Public Administration Clearing House.

Wenger, Dennis E. 1978. Community Response to Disaster: Functional and Structural Alterations. In *Disasters: Theory and Research*, edited by Enrico L. Quarantelli, 17–47. Beverly Hills: Sage.

Wilson, Robert N. 1962. Disaster and Mental Health. In *Man and Society in Disaster*, edited by George W. Baker and Dwight W. Chapman, 124–50. New York: Basic Books.

Winter, Marcus. 1988. Periodo Prehispanico. In *Historia de la Cuestión Agraria Mexicana, Estado de Oaxaca*, edited by Reticia Renia. Mexico: Juan Pablos, S.A.

Wolf, Charles P. 1979. *Quality of Life, Concept and Measurement: A Preliminary Bibliography*. Monticello, Ill.: Vance Bibliographies.

Wolf, Fredric M. 1986. *Meta-Analysis: Quantitative Methods for Research Synthesis*. Beverly Hills: Sage.

Wolf, Scott. 1978. *Measurement and Analysis of Progress at the Local Level*. Geneva: United Nations Research Institute for Social Development.

World Bank. 1984. *World Development Report, 1984*. New York: Oxford University Press.

World Resources Institute. 1990. *World Resources, 1990–91*. New York: Oxford University Press.

Wright, James D., Peter H. Rossi, Sonia R. Wright, and Eleanor Weber-Burdin. 1979. *After the Clean-Up: Long-Range Effects of Natural Disasters*. Beverly Hills: Sage.

Zeller, Richard A., and Edward G. Carmines. 1980. *Measurement in the Social Sciences*. New York: Cambridge University Press.

Index

157